F
a
4   ...rue Walks   m
                                  r

The author and publisher have made every effort to ensure that the information in this publication is accurate, and accept no responsibility whatsoever for any loss, injury or inconvenience experienced by any person or persons whilst using this book.

published by
pocket mountains ltd
The Old Church, Annanside, Moffat, DG10 9HB
pocketmountains.com

ISBN: 978-1-907025-45-7

Text and photography copyright © 2016 Keith Fergus

The right of Keith Fergus to be identified as the Author of this work has been asserted by him in accordance with the Copyright, Designs and Patents Act 1988

A catalogue record for this book is available from the British Library

Contains Ordnance Survey data © Crown copyright and database right 2016, supported by out of copyright mapping from 1945-1961

Printed in Poland

Introduction

Think of Lochaber and mountains will probably spring to mind – lots of them, big ones too, including the biggest of them all, Ben Nevis. The Mamores, Beinn a' Chrulaiste, Sgorr na Ciche (better known as the Pap of Glencoe) and the iconic Buachaille Etive Mor are just a few of the other peaks that make Lochaber so venerated by hillwalkers and climbers.

Yet it offers much more than mountain scenery. The region takes in the wild and spectacular Ardgour and Ardnamurchan Peninsulas, the natural grandeur of Creag Meagaidh, a section of the Great Glen and the magical *Rathad an Eilean*, the Road to the Isles, which threads its way through the romantic landscape between Fort William and Mallaig.

As it moves around the region, this guidebook takes you on a journey that explores woodland, lochs, waterfalls, canal, moorland and coast, allowing fascinating insights into Lochaber's history, geology and flora and fauna – as well as some of the finest beaches this side of the Caribbean.

There have been calls for Lochaber to be designated Scotland's third National Park – in walking across this landscape it would be hard to disagree with this assertion.

History

The history of Lochaber will forever be linked with its most unruly periods – the Jacobite Uprising of 1745 and the Massacre of Glencoe, which took place on 13 February 1692 and saw the vicious slaying of 38 members of the MacDonald clan after they failed to pledge allegiance (many would say rightly so) to King William and his government regime in London.

This atrocity caused outrage in Scotland, becoming a potent symbol of anti-government propaganda, one that would help fuel the fire of Jacobite sympathies and the Uprisings of 1715 and 1745.

The most famous individual involved in the 1745 rebellion was Charles Edward Stuart, better known now as Bonnie Prince Charlie. At Glenfinnan he symbolically raised his royal standard to begin the revolt against the British monarchy that would end in failure on 16 April 1746 at the Battle of Culloden.

Perhaps unsurprisingly given the hostile mountainous terrain, the early influence of humans on Lochaber's landscape was minimal and there is relatively little evidence of ancient sites – one of the few examples is the Iron Age fort of Dun Deardail above Glen Nevis.

A number of place names in the region have Pictish origins, unusual for the West of Scotland when the influence of the Picts was so much greater in North East Scotland. Lochaber itself means 'Area of the Loch Confluence', probably referring to the meeting of Loch Eil and Loch Linnhe, while the Norse influence can also be seen in names like Mallaig and Arisaig. However, the dominant language and culture was Gaelic and the majority of river, loch and mountain designations stem from this poetic tongue.

In recent centuries, crofting and fishing have been important in building communities such as Arisaig, Mallaig and many of the tiny settlements along the peninsulas of Ardgour and Ardnamurchan.

Early industry has also had a part to play. The village of Strontian, on the banks of Loch Sunart, developed through mining during the 18th century and the slate quarries at Ballachulish roofed many of Scotland's buildings while the aluminium smelters at both Fort William and Kinlochleven exploited the local landscape.

Today, Lochaber's landscape is still central to its popularity and economic success. Low-level and mountain walking are complemented by the long-distance walking routes, the West Highland Way and the Great Glen Way, both of which start or finish within its boundaries.

Cycling, sailing, skiing and wildlife watching are also key outdoor activities and Fort William lies at the heart of the area branded 'the Outdoor Capital of the UK'. Other villages such as Glencoe, Kinlochleven, Spean Bridge, Kilchoan and Mallaig make excellent bases for exploring different parts of the region.

The natural environment

The geology of Lochaber is what makes it such a compelling place in which to walk. For example, much of the western part of the Ardnamurchan Peninsula was formed through volcanic activity – the ancient ring structures that remain have, in particular, drawn geologists from all over the world.

Much of Glen Nevis and Glen Coe were also formed through volcanic activity about 430 million years ago, shaping their iconic peaks. Lochaber's landform began to take shape around this time when the two continents of Laurentia (which now makes up most of Canada) and Avalonia (carrying England and part of Northern Europe) collided to form the Great Glen Fault.

This extends for 190km from the Moray Firth to the Firth of Lorn at the mouth of Loch Linnhe and contains the deep freshwater lochs of Ness, Oich and Lochy – today all three are linked by the engineering feat of the Caledonian Canal.

Around 20,000 years ago, when Scotland was at its coldest, only the summit of Ben Nevis poked above the ice pack while much of Lochaber remained under an ice sheet until 11,500 years ago when it began to grind the mountains and scour the glens. This weathering and erosion met its match with the more resistant granite peaks of Ben Nevis, the Aonach Eagach Ridge and the Mamores range.

Lochaber also has a number of fjords (better known as sea lochs) characteristic of land that has been subject to glaciation, including Loch Sunart, Loch Nevis and Scotland's longest sea loch, Loch Linnhe.

All of this points to an outstanding geological heritage that has seen Lochaber designated as one of only three geoparks in Scotland (the other two are the North West Highlands and Shetland Geoparks).

The wildlife and marine life thriving in and around this diverse landscape is second to none and includes golden and white-tailed sea eagle, puffin, storm petrel red deer, otter, bottle-nosed dolphin and minke whale.

Remnants of the ancient Atlantic Oakwood that once covered much of Europe's west coast can be found in Lochaber and among the varied plantlife that this region sustains are many mosses, lichens and a vast selection of wildflowers.

How to use this guide

Almost all of the walks in this guide can be completed within half a day, leaving plenty of time to explore the natural attractions and historic sites you encounter along the way. Many of the walks are accessible by bus or train, mainly from the Central Belt and from Fort William. Basic public transport information is included in this guide, but details and times can change so please check these before you set out (travelinescotland.com).

The majority of the routes are low-level and take advantage of the excellent network of paths found here. It is not advisable to stray from the routes onto farmland or near exposed cliffs and, where livestock is present, dogs must always be kept on leads.

A few of the routes cross steep hill or mountain terrain where good mapreading and navigation skills are necessary in poor weather. Winter walking brings distinct challenges, particularly the limited daylight hours, whilst strong winds along the coast and over higher ground can occur throughout the year.

Preparation for a walk should begin before you set out, and your choice of route should reflect your fitness, the conditions underfoot and the regional weather forecasts (mwis.org.uk).

Even in summer, warm, waterproof clothing is advisable and footwear that is comfortable and supportive with good grips is a must.

None of the hillwalks or longer routes in this guide should be attempted without the relevant OS map or equivalent at 1:50,000 (or 1:25,000) – and you should know how to navigate using an OS map and compass.

Under the Land Reform (Scotland) Act of 2003, there is a right of public access to the countryside of Scotland for recreational purposes. This right depends on whether it is exercised responsibly, while landowners have an obligation not to unreasonably prevent or deter those seeking access. The responsibilities of the public and land managers are set out in the Scottish Outdoor Access Code (outdooraccess-scotland.com).

Glencoe needs little introduction for walkers. Scotland's most famous glen is renowned for the mountains that rise steeply, contributing to a brooding atmosphere that is all its own.

Only a two-hour drive from Glasgow and Inverness, Glencoe is incredibly popular all year round. It is seen by many as the spiritual home of Scottish mountaineering and played a pivotal role in the sport's popularisation in the 1930s.

Buachaille Etive Mor, Bidean nam Bian and the Aonach Eagach are the icons of the glen and see walkers' boots on their slopes almost every day of the year, giving the glen a deserved reputation as a mountaineering playground.

However, it is the peaks of Beinn a' Chrulaiste, Am Bodach and Sgorr na Ciche (the Pap of Glencoe) that arguably make the most inspiring venues for surveying their loftier cousins. Away from the heights altogether are many lower level but often equally dramatic locations.

One of the more challenging of these is Coire Gabhail, The Lost Valley, on a route as thrilling as any of its more precipitous neighbours.

More simple circuitous routes can be found at the beautiful Glencoe Lochan and An Torr.

One of the most scenic stretches of the West Highland Way crosses through Glencoe, and several walks in this chapter share sections with this long-distance route, including one from the Ladies Scottish Climbing Club's home at Blackrock Cottage.

There is an almost palpable sense of history in the glen, and the memory of the infamous Massacre of Glencoe seems to reside in the very landscape itself. Tangible evidence of a more recent past can be seen at Ballachulish and Kinlochleven, with walks that take in an old slate quarry, aluminium works and two different aspects of Loch Leven.

The Three Sisters from Am Bodach ▸

Glencoe

1 Blackrock to Ba and back 8
March along an old military road for
commanding views over Rannoch Moor

**2 Beinn a' Chrulaiste from
the Kings House** 10
A steep climb rewarded with a
revealing overview of Glencoe

3 Beyond the Devil's Staircase 12
Step up for a challenging high-level trek
that sets off on the West Highland Way

4 Am Bodach 14
Scramble up the peak that marks the
start of the famous Aonach Eagach

5 The Lost Valley 16
Lose yourself in a glorious gorge and
discover the secret glen that may have
saved lives in the Massacre of Glencoe

6 An Torr and Signal Rock 18
Immerse yourself in clan history on
a visit to a famous lookout point

7 The Pap of Glencoe 20
Soak up the scenery from this
distinctive peak above Loch Leven

8 Glencoe Lochan 22
Stroll through a woodland idyll
with plenty of wildlife interest

9 Ballachulish to Loch Leven 24
Walk through an historic slate quarry
for a peaceful lochside panorama

10 The Brecklet Trail 26
Follow an easy woodland trail through
the industrial heritage of Ballachulish

**11 Kinlochleven and
the Grey Mare's Tail** 28
Visit a celebrated waterfall and return
along the West Highland Way

Blackrock to Ba and back

Distance 8.25km **Time** 2 hours 30
Terrain moorland paths and tracks, short
section where path is indistinct
Map OS Explorer 384 **Access** regular buses
from Glasgow and Fort William to
Glencoe Mountain Resort road end
(limited parking here; drivers park at
Mountain Resort)

**Bask in the breathtaking views on this
relatively simple route that utilises an
old military road above Rannoch Moor
to reach the ruin of Ba Cottage. Return
along the West Highland Way to
Blackrock Cottage.**

Start from Blackrock Cottage, a little
way down the signed Mountain Resort
track off the A82 at the head of Glencoe.
Blackrock holds a scenic position a stone's
throw from the mighty Buachaille Etive

Mor and the craggy slopes of Meall
a'Bhuiridh and Creise. It is owned by
the Ladies Scottish Climbing Club, which
was founded near Killin in 1908, making
it the world's oldest all-women's
mountaineering club still in existence.

Take the West Highland Way track
opposite Blackrock Cottage, then keep
right at a fork just before a little wooden
hut. A wide stony track climbs gently
beneath the slopes of Meall a'Bhuiridh
(which translates from Gaelic as 'Peak of
the Roaring') and crosses a stone bridge
over a burn.

Leaving the West Highland Way, turn
right at a marker, then immediately left
onto a narrow path, an old General
Caulfeild military road that ran from Fort
William to Tyndrum and was constructed
between 1751 and 1752. The path, which

can be a little boggy at times, climbs gradually southeast over heathery hill slopes with views opening out across Rannoch Moor as far as Schiehallion's conical summit.

It soon widens to a stony track and crosses a couple of small burns to reach its highest point at around 500m above sea level. Here, the view extends across Rannoch Moor's flat mattress to Loch Ba, Lochan na Stainge, Lochan na h-Achlaise, Beinn Achaladair, Beinn an Dothaidh and the Blackmount.

A narrower and sometimes vague path now begins to descend gently but soon broadens to a grassy track, dropping south and then southeast to meet the West Highland Way beside a stone bridge over a fast-flowing burn.

Turn right to cross the bridge and follow the West Highland Way a short distance. After crossing a bridge over the Allt Creagan nam Meann, turn right to soon reach the lonely ruin of Ba Cottage, which sits beneath the steep slopes of Clach Leathad in a spectacular setting for a break. There is a good chance of spotting red deer on the hillside.

Return to the West Highland Way and retrace your steps, passing the junction with the military road. Stick with the Way as the track steepens. A memorial cairn dedicated to Peter Fleming, charismatic travel writer, adventurer and brother of

James Bond author Ian Fleming, who died here in 1971 while shooting grouse, marks the top of the climb.

It is now a simple descent along the track. The view is no less impressive with the Mamores, Beinn a' Chrulaiste and Buachaille Etive Mor filling the landscape ahead. Eventually you regain the outward route beside the military road. From here, retrace your steps to Blackrock Cottage.

Beinn a' Chrulaiste from the Kings House

Distance 9.5km **Time** 4 hours
Terrain mountain paths, some sections
of pathless terrain; fairly steep ascents,
one sharp descent **Map** OS Explorer 384
Access regular buses from Glasgow, Fort
William and Uig to Kings House Hotel
road end; permission must be sought if
parking at Kings House Hotel

A climb to the top of Beinn a' Chrulaiste
is the perfect way to experience what are
arguably the best views of Glencoe. Many
of the mountains here hold technical
difficulties and are suitable for only
experienced walkers, but the slopes of
this peak are more forgiving and the
summit is generally within reach of fit
walkers. The route crosses pathless
terrain, however, so map-reading skills
are essential in poor visibility. Part of the
descent is through craggy outcrops
where extra care is required.

Walk through the Kings House Hotel
car park, to the right of the hotel, which
dates from the 1750s and was built as a
barracks and safe house for travellers.
Once across a bridge over the River Etive,
follow a single-track road to a junction
and turn right through a gate signposted
'Public Path to Rannoch'.

Immediately turn left, cross a narrow
burn and then follow an indistinct path
north over boggy moorland. The trail
becomes a little more obvious as it
approaches the clear waters of the
Allt a' Bhalaich, one of the main early
tributaries of the River Etive.

A decent path now climbs gently along
the river's west bank, steepening a little
as it rises north towards Coire Bhalach,
with the craggy eastern shoulder of Beinn
a' Chrulaiste above. Eventually, the path
leads more steeply above the water as it
cascades down through a rocky gorge.

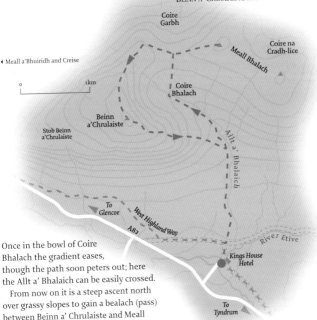

◄ Meall a'Bhuiridh and Creise

Once in the bowl of Coire Bhalach the gradient eases, though the path soon peters out; here the Allt a' Bhalaich can be easily crossed.

From now on it is a steep ascent north over grassy slopes to gain a bealach (pass) between Beinn a' Chrulaiste and Meall Bhalach. Go right and climb steadily east across open moorland onto Meall Bhalach with its view out over Blackwater Reservoir to the Mamores and beyond to the distinctive flat top of Ben Nevis.

Retrace your steps to the bealach where a gradual incline up firm, stony ground proceeds west and then southwest along an obvious broad ridge. A final steep pull to the south attains Beinn a' Chrulaiste's 857m top and a panorama that includes Meall a'Bhuiridh, Creise and the high peaks around Bridge of Orchy. It also presents what is possibly the best view of the Buachaille's iconic profile, with the

bowl of Coire na Tulaich cut deep into the slopes of this most celebrated of Scottish mountains.

From the summit, descend steep ground southeast and then east. The terrain is pathless and drops down through craggy outcrops – although not difficult, care should be taken on this descent. Once below the crags, continue down grassy slopes to the Allt a' Bhalaich.

Go right and retrace your steps to the Kings House Hotel, enjoying the many tumbling waterfalls and the magnificent outlook to Meall a'Bhuiridh as you go.

11

Beyond the Devil's Staircase

Distance 13km **Time** 6 hours (round trip)
Terrain mountain paths, some of which
can be indistinct. Several steep ascents
and descents **Map** OS Explorer 384
Access regular buses from Glasgow and
Fort William to Altnafeadh

This walk, which starts out on the
West Highland Way, incorporates the
Devil's Staircase and Am Bodach in an
exhilarating high-level ridgewalk that
encompasses all the diversity of Glencoe.
It ends where the infamous Aonach
Eagach begins but with few of that
ridgewalk's difficulties or exposure,
despite some steep sections of its own.

The walk begins at Altnafeadh, the
usual start point for those climbing
Buachaille Etive Mor (the Buachaille),
which rises majestically across the glen
from the banks of the River Coupall.

Take the West Highland Way track
that zigzags its way north up the Devil's
Staircase. It is thought that this steep
ascent was given its name by soldiers
transporting building materials as part
of General Wade's road network. It's a
tough pull, though the sweeping vista
of Stob Dearg, Buachaille Etive Mor's
eastern Munro peak, is a good excuse
for a break.

As you might expect from a climb whose
summit sits just short of 550m, the views
are far-reaching with the Buachaille at your
back and the full length of the Mamores
forming a defensive wall ahead. Beyond,
Ben Nevis towers above everything.

From the top, turn left onto grassy
slopes for a steady rise west onto Stob
Mhic Mhartuin and then more steeply
onto Sron a' Choire Odhair-bhig. The
prospect now extends over Blackwater

◄ The Mamores from Stob Mhic Mhartuin

Reservoir (when the dam was built between 1904 and 1909, the workers also used the Devil's Staircase as a means of getting to the Kings House Hotel, where their wages were spent) and Leum Uilleim to Scheihallion's perfectly symmetrical outline. It is now a spectacular high-level ridgewalk all the way to Am Bodach.

A faint path continues west, clinging to the edge of the ridge and climbing to an unnamed peak at 903m. Here, the famed Three Sisters of Glencoe and the imposing slopes of Bidean nam Bian dominate the view, whilst Kinlochleven sits way below to the north. A steep drop down and around bouldery slopes leads to a bealach

below Sron Garbh. From here, a traverse of grassy slopes gains the ridge between Sron Garbh and Am Bodach. A steep ascent through some rocky outcrops (no scrambling involved) brings you out at Am Bodach's 943m summit.

The notorious but classic ridgeline of the Aonach Eagach stretches for some 2km, drawing the eye on from here to Beinn a'Bheithir above Ballachulish.

The most straightforward return journey is to retrace your steps to Altnafeadh. The steep climb back over the unnamed peak is the sting in the tail but, with such a magnificent ridge and views, you may not even notice.

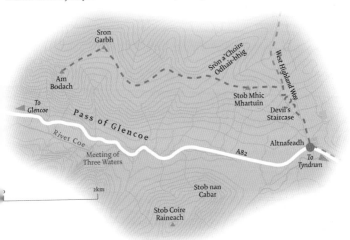

Am Bodach

Distance 7.25km **Time** 4 hours (round trip)
Terrain mountain paths with steep
ascents and descents; light scrambling
may be required **Map** OS Explorer 384
Access regular buses from Glasgow and
Fort William to the car park

The infamous Aonach Eagach Ridge is
beyond the capabilities of many
hillwalkers, its jagged pinnacles and
extreme exposure providing a real
mountaineering test. However, Am
Bodach, the Aonach Eagach's easternmost
top, is far more attainable and gives a real
sense of the challenge that awaits those
attempting the ridge. There are a number
of steep ascents and descents throughout
this route and in wet or wintry conditions
considerable care needs to be taken.

The name Am Bodach translates from
Gaelic as 'the Old Man'. There are many Am
Bodachs in Scottish hill nomenclature and,
invariably, where you have 'the Old Man',
'the Old Woman' (A'Chailleach) will not be
far away. In this case, she sits just a little to
the east, above Allt-na-reigh.

Start from the car park just west of Allt-
na-reigh and take the path at its right
corner. Immediately a steep climb takes
you east and then north above Glencoe
and the sparkling waters of the Allt-na-
reigh. As the ascent continues, views of
Aonach Dubh, Gearr Aonach and Beinn
Fhada (known collectively as the Three
Sisters) and Bidean nam Bian open up
across the glen to your left.

Winding its way up above fairly steep
slopes in a northwesterly direction the

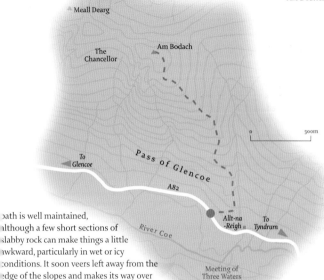

path is well maintained, although a few short sections of slabby rock can make things a little awkward, particularly in wet or icy conditions. It soon veers left away from the edge of the slopes and makes its way over a rocky shelf, after which a stepped section helps with the steep gradient.

The crags above look almost impenetrable, but in a while the path does climb through them without any major difficulties. Eventually it runs beneath the first main crag where your efforts are compensated by an uninterrupted view along the Pass of Glencoe to Loch Achtriochtan and then Beinn a'Bheithir. Across the glen, the craggy buttresses of Stob Coire nan Lochan draw the eye to the flowing contours of Bidean nam Bian.

As the route heads up through the crags, some simple scrambling may be necessary, but the path is clear throughout. The steep gradient means height is gained very quickly and so, in what seems like no time,

you reach Am Bodach's southeast ridge.

The gradient eases a little and a final uneventful segment of the ascent continues onto the airy 943m summit of Am Bodach. The Aonach Eagach's eastern peak of Meall Dearg rises a short distance to the northwest but to reach it involves a slightly awkward descent.

Therefore, Am Bodach may well be the limit for most, but there are few better vantage points to linger on – the prospect along the Aonach's 2km ridge is breathtaking, as is the view north across the long ridgeline of the Mamores to Ben Nevis.

The descent is made by the same route and real care should be taken throughout.

◀ Aonach Eagach from Am Bodach

The Lost Valley

Distance 4.5km **Time** 2 hours 30 (round trip) **Terrain** rocky glen paths with some light scrambling. Awkward river crossing by stepping stones, which may be impassable in spate **Map** OS Explorer 384 **Access** regular buses from Glasgow and Fort William to the car park

One of Glencoe's greatest surprises is that ranked among its best walks is a low-level route through an enclosed gorge. This out-and-back walk climbs alongside the picturesque Allt Coire Gabhail, eventually opening out into the spectacular Coire Gabhail, *aka* The Lost Valley. The terrain underfoot can be awkward with steep drops running near the edge of the path, so real care should be taken throughout. The fast-flowing river also has to be forded twice and may be impassable in spate. But even if you turn back here, this walk will live long in the memory.

Start from the large car park on the southern side of the A82 in the Pass of Glencoe (this is the bigger and more easterly of two car parks). Drop down the path into the glen, heading southeast with an outlook to the Three Sisters of Glencoe.

Once down a flight of steps, turn left to take a path across a wooden footbridge over the River Coe. After a short but slightly awkward climb over rocky slabs, a gradual rise along the path passes through a gate. This marks the start of a steady ascent southwest, beneath the distinctive northeast crag of Gearr Aonach.

The climb then winds high above the narrow gorge of the Allt Coire Gabhail through birch woodland. Soon the path runs along the edge of the gorge with exposed drops down to the left – eyes should be trained on where you are walking, especially when crossing a couple of rocky shelves.

16

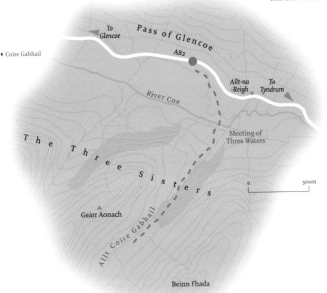

Beyond a dramatic waterfall, hands may be required when climbing over a rocky section or two. The gorge is now enveloped by steep, near-vertiginous slopes with the route running alongside crystal waters. Boulders of all shapes and sizes litter the glen; it is simply breathtaking.

In a while, the walk passes to the right of an enormous boulder, after which you reach another waterfall just before a high wall of boulders. Keep left by the river here and, if the water level is low, make the reasonably simple crossing by stepping stones. However, if the river is in spate, it would be wise to conclude the walk at this point and retrace your steps to Glencoe.

On the opposite bank, a rough, stony path climbs steadily with the water to your right. After negotiating a tricky rock slab, the going much improves and there is a steady uphill incline to soon cross a narrow burn. A short climb and then gradual descent leads into the freedom of Coire Gabhail and its quite unexpected sense of space. This natural amphitheatre is bounded by the great mountains of Gearr Aonach, Beinn Fhada and the monumental Bidean nam Bian.

The descent is made by retracing your steps, taking care at the awkward sections and relishing the views across Glencoe to the great wall of the Aonach Eagach.

An Torr and Signal Rock

Distance 4.25km **Time** 1 hour 30
Terrain single-track road, woodland paths
Map OS Explorer 384 **Access** regular buses
from Glasgow and Fort William to the
Clachaig Inn road end

History permeates the landscape
of Glencoe and this fascinating walk
visits Signal Rock, believed to be where
the glen's most infamous event, the
brutal Massacre of Glencoe, began.
The route starts from Loch Achtriochtan,
where there is a small car park, and
then makes its way through the
woodland of An Torr.

From the west end of Loch Achtriochtan,
a view of the length of the Aonach Eagach,
one of Britain's most famous mountain
ridges, unfolds along the glen. Starting at
the car park here, carefully cross the A82,
turn left and follow this over the River Coe.

Take the path from the roadside which
heads west between the river and the A82
to reach the An Torr car park.

Walk across this to join a path, which
drops down over a footbridge and then
crosses another bridge over a fast-flowing
section of the River Coe.

After this, the path splits. Keep left and
climb steps, bearing left through a gate at a
yellow/black/blue waymark into An Torr.
Native tree species found here include
birch, Scots pine, rowan and alder, with
plenty of wildlife for the eagle-eyed to look
out for, including roe deer, tawny owl,
woodpecker, red squirrel and the elusive
pine marten.

Carry on to a fork, where you go left
(blue/black waymark), soon dropping to a
junction. Turn right here and continue to
the next junction where a left turn now
follows blue waymarks.

◄ Loch Achtriochtan

Once through a gate, the path descends and then rises to a three-way junction. Go straight on and climb steps to gain Signal Rock. Narrow steps lead to the top with views along the glen.

The Gaelic name for Signal Rock is *Tom a' Ghrianain*, meaning 'Hill of the Sun'. As well as being a meeting point for the MacDonalds of Glencoe in times of strife, legend has it that the Campbells lit a fire here to signal the start of the Glencoe Massacre on 13 February 1692. There is no definitive evidence for either. However, it is thought that Tom a' Ghrianan may have been a site of pre-Christian worship where thousands of years ago people worshipped their gods.

Retrace your steps to the fork with the blue/black waymark and turn left. The path soon drops down over a narrow footbridge, then climbs steeply up the wooded hillside. After a gradual descent, another steep rise leads to a fork. Keep left to continue to a junction at an 'An Torr' sign. Turn left, walk down through two gates and out of An Torr onto a minor road.

Go right to pass the welcoming Clachaig Inn, an historic watering hole that has refreshed tired walkers for more than 200 years and is rooted in the history of Scottish mountaineering.

Carry on along the minor road for 750m, with the landscape dominated by Bidean nam Bian and neighbouring peaks, to reach the A82. Carefully cross the road back to Loch Achtriochtan.

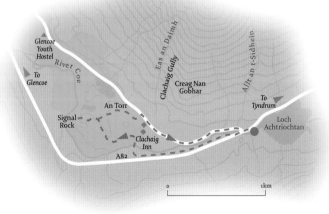

The Pap of Glencoe

Distance 7.25km **Time** 4 hours (round trip)
Terrain single-track road, hill paths. Some
steep sections **Map** OS Explorer 384
Access regular buses from Glasgow and
Fort William to Glencoe Village

Sgorr na Ciche (known to most as the
Pap of Glencoe) is a much-loved landmark
that overlooks the south bank of Loch
Leven at the foot of Glencoe. It translates
from Gaelic as 'Peak of the Breast' and
when looking along Loch Leven from
Ballachulish Bridge it is easy to appreciate
why. A good path climbs onto its 742m top
for a remarkable panorama.

Facing the thatched Glencoe Folk
Museum turn right to walk along the main
street and across the Bridge of Coe, which
spans the river after which it is named.
A single-track road now heads southeast
through woodland, hugging the banks of
the River Coe.

After around 750m, pass a car park (an
alternative start point) where a path now
runs to the left of the road for a short spell.
The road is then followed again but, just
after passing the entrance to 'Laraichean'
on the left, turn left to pass through two
consecutive farm gates.

Follow the path beyond as it climbs
to a junction near some waterworks.
Go right here onto another path that
crosses a footbridge over a burn. With
the steep slopes of Sgorr na Ciche

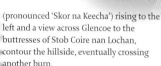

(pronounced 'Skor na Keecha') rising to the left and a view across Glencoe to the buttresses of Stob Coire nan Lochan, contour the hillside, eventually crossing another burn.

After this, the path narrows a little and then begins to climb northeast. It is a steady pull with views opening out all the time. Although the path can be a little boggy at times the going is generally good.

At last, the gradient eases a little. Stick to the main path, ignoring one that bears east towards Sgorr nam Fiannaidh, to gain a bealach between this peak and Sgorr na Ciche. When the path reaches the lower summit slopes of Sgorr na Ciche, it begins to climb quite steeply over rocky ground, though you should not encounter any difficulties.

The final few metres traverse the Pap's eastern flank before swinging to the left to gain the summit where there is plenty of space to enjoy the sweeping panorama. Across Loch Leven rises the wall of the Mamores with Binnein Mor and Am Bodach (which is loftier than its namesake in Glencoe) the particular standouts. The village of Kinlochleven also lies some distance below. To the west, Ballachulish is dwarfed by Beinn a'Bheithir, which is comprised of the two Munro peaks of Sgorr Dhonuill and Sgorr Dhearg, with the scene stretching across Loch Linnhe to the mountains of Ardgour.

Once you've had your fill of the views, the simplest return is to carefully drop back down to the bealach and then retrace the route into Glencoe Village.

◀ Looking down on Loch Leven

Glencoe Lochan

**Distance 3.75km Time 1 hour
Terrain paths and tracks, one steep
descent, gentle climbs Map OS Explorer
384 Access regular buses from Glasgow
and Fort William to Glencoe Village**

**This straightforward walk heads through
attractive woodland on the outskirts of
Glencoe Village before looping around
Glencoe Lochan. Wildlife abounds within
the woods, making this a wonderful walk
for all ages and abilities.**

The walk begins at the Glencoe Folk
Museum, which details the fascinating
history of Glencoe and North Lorn (open
from April to October).

Facing the museum, turn right to walk
along the main street and over the river on
the Bridge of Coe. Take the second road on
the left, signposted for Glencoe Lochan.

This rises gently through mixed woodland
to a fork where you keep right and
continue to a car park.

Cross through here, then take the left-
hand path into the trees. The businessman
and philanthropist Lord Strathcona, who
was born in the Moray village of Forres in
1820 but emigrated to Canada at the age of
18, planted many of the conifers that
punctuate the woodland around Glencoe
Lochan. He was in charge of the Hudson
Bay Company for much of his life, but
returned to Scotland during the 1890s with
his Canadian wife, Isabella, and acquired
Glencoe Estate.

However, Isabella felt so homesick that
her husband tried to recreate the Canadian
forest environment for her by planting
many trees throughout the estate.
Lord Strathcona died in London in 1914,

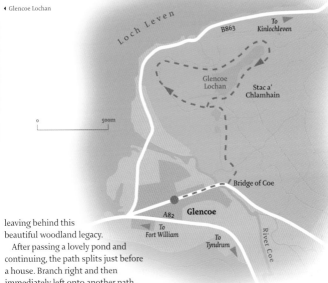

◄ Glencoe Lochan

leaving behind this beautiful woodland legacy.

After passing a lovely pond and continuing, the path splits just before a house. Branch right and then immediately left onto another path. This climbs gradually into dense pine woodland where you may spot stonechat, woodpecker and roe deer. At the top of the incline, an easy section precedes a short steep descent. A viewpoint on the left gives a sweeping outlook across Loch Leven to Beinn a'Bheithir.

The path continues easily eastwards, eventually reaching Glencoe Lochan. Turn left to follow a solid path clockwise around this peaceful location where you can look out for goldeneye, goosander and red-breasted merganser amongst other birds. Here, at the heart of a magnificent natural amphitheatre, you are also well placed to appreciate some of Scotland's finest mountains, such as Beinn a'Bheithir and Sgorr na Ciche (better known as the Pap of Glencoe), rising steeply beyond the wooded confines. The path is easily navigated around the lochan to reach a fork beside a fisherman's hut.

Carry straight on away from the lochan, then go left where the path splits again. Zigzag down through woodland and back to the car park, retracing your steps from here to Glencoe Village.

Ballachulish to Loch Leven

Distance 2.5km Time 1 hour
Terrain paths, minor roads
Map OS Explorer 384 Access regular
buses from Glasgow and Fort William
to Ballachulish

This is a straightforward and scenic
walk around the historic slate quarries
of Ballachulish, where tangible evidence
of the industry still exists, as does a
surprising variety of wildlife. The route
also reaches Loch Leven with its stunning
mountain backdrop.

From Ballachulish Visitor Centre car park,
walk through the gap between the centre
and the public toilets and then cross Park
Road to Ballachulish Slate Quarry directly
opposite. Beyond the left-hand gate, keep
left along a prepared path and walk
beneath the vertical cliffs of the quarry.
This takes you past two ponds on your
right which were formed when the quarries

closed and are today teeming with birds.

The quarry dates from the late 1600s and
had its heyday in the mid-1800s when
millions of slates were quarried every year.
The high quality of the slate meant it was
used in many buildings across Scotland,
including those designed by Charles Rennie
Mackintosh who loved the colour of
Ballachulish slate. The quarry closed in 1955.

At a junction, cross a track and then turn
right to follow a path alongside a pond into
woodland. Continue until you regain the
outward path, turning left to exit the quarry.
Just beyond the gates, turn right onto a path
which leads alongside Park Road and then
swings right beside the A82 to reach the
renowned slate arch. Built in 1822, the arch
stands more than 24m in height and was
one of two such arches that helped move
slate from the upper quarry to the shore.
It is now a Scheduled Monument.

Retrace your steps along the A82, cross

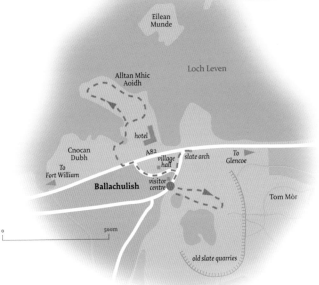

to the opposite side of Park Road and return towards the visitor centre. Before you get there, turn right at the junction (this is also Park Road) to pass the village hall. Follow this road as it heads down beneath the A82 and carries on past a car park on the right to reach one on the left beside a hotel. To the left, by a slipway, are several old slate boatsheds.

Cross the car park to pick up a grassy path which leads clockwise around a little peninsula along the shores of Loch Leven. Views extend to Ballachulish Bridge which links North and South Ballachulish and opened in 1975 to replace a ferry service that had run for nearly 250 years.

At the end of the peninsula, turn sharp right and follow a path above Loch Leven, visited by arctic tern, cormorant, oystercatcher, storm petrel and Manx shearwater. Out on the water is Eilean Munde, home to a chapel built by St Fintan Mundus who settled here from Iona during the 7th century. The island also contains a graveyard used by the Stewarts of Ballachulish, the MacDonalds of Glencoe and the Camerons of Calart. Nearby is Eilean a' Chomhriadh, 'the Island of Discussion'. This was used to deliberate on local disputes such as land ownership.

Keep along the path but, as it drops down towards the hotel, bear right and return to the car park. Turn left to retrace your steps to Ballachulish.

The Brecklet Trail

Distance 3.25km Time 1 hour 30
Terrain paths, minor roads
Map OS Explorer 384 Access regular buses
from Glasgow and Fort William to
Ballachulish

The Brecklet Trail climbs through the
attractive woodland to the south of
Ballachulish and the village's renowned
slate quarries. The views alone make this
a worthwhile journey, with the return
travelling through Brecklet, the oldest
part of Ballachulish.

From Ballachulish Visitor Centre car
park, walk through the gap between the
centre and the public toilets and then cross
Park Road to Ballachulish Slate Quarry
opposite. Beyond the gate, turn right onto
the Brecklet Trail and follow a path lined
with alder, birch, willow, ash and rowan as
it rises steeply with views over the quarry.

The slate was formed when layer upon
layer of mud compacted over millions of

years. Ballachulish slate was renowned
for its high quality and was used in many
buildings across Scotland. This was one
of the major centres of slate quarrying
during its 19th-century heyday with almost
the whole community involved in the
industry; many families living in the
village today are direct descendants of
those who once worked here.

As the path leads onto open hillside,
views open out across Loch Leven and Loch
Linnhe to the craggy Ardgour mountains.
Beinn a'Bheithir rears sharply to the west
of Ballachulish and dominates the
immediate landscape. Carry on along the
path as it zigzags up to a gate.

Beyond this, turn left to follow another
path on a steep incline along the edge of
woodland. It then swings right into the
trees and up to a junction. A left turn leads
the short way to a great viewpoint.

Return to the main path and continue
straight on through the woodland, with

▾ Loch Leven from the Brecklet Trail

the climb now easing. In a while, the path turns left up a short steep slope to a waymark. Go right for a steady zigzag descent, passing through the ruins of an old settlement.

The path now drops down, crossing a couple of sparkling burns, with waterfalls cascading through the woodland. Among the many birds you may spot here are siskin, coal-tit, redpoll and goldcrest, while on the ground plantlife such as wood sorrel, wood sage, lichen and golden saxifrage thrive seasonally in the damp climate.

At a T-junction, go right and follow a track through a gate onto a single-track road which passes through Brecklet with its scattering of houses and two churches, St Munda's and St Mun's, both of which are named after St Fintan Mundus, who settled on Eilean Munde from Iona during the 7th century.

Follow the road alongside the fast-flowing River Laroch which tumbles down through Gleann an Fhiodh and into Loch Leven. At Laroch Beag, beside an old stone bridge spanning the river, turn right and continue back to Park Road, turning right again to return to the visitor centre.

Kinlochleven and the Grey Mare's Tail

Distance 5.5km **Time** 2 hours
Terrain woodland, riverbank, hill paths
and pavement **Map** OS Explorer 392
Access regular buses from Glencoe and
Fort William to Kinlochleven

Translating from the Gaelic *Ceann Loch Liobhann* as 'the Head of Loch Leven', Kinlochleven sits a little off the tourist highway between Glencoe and Fort William but is a hub for walkers heading through the village on the West Highland Way, as well as climbers visiting the renowned Ice Factor climbing centre. Another of its highlights is the dramatic Grey Mare's Tail, one of Scotland's most impressive waterfalls.

From the village centre, follow Lochaber Road (B863) across a bridge over the River Leven, then turn right onto Kearan Road. At its end, go right onto Wades Road and then take a woodland path just to the right of St Paul's Church, entering the Mamore Estate. Where the path branches, keep left for a gradual ascent to another fork. Go left here to drop down steps and cross a footbridge over a burn.

Walk left and follow a rough path for a short distance to reach the Grey Mare's Tail, which drops the Allt Coire nam Ba some 50 vertical metres into a narrow wooded gorge, creating a dramatic scene.

Return to the bridge, but don't cross; instead carry straight on along a path which soon swings left at a waymark. It's a steep pull through the woodland with views now opening out over Kinlochleven and the old aluminium smelter that was instrumental in the village's development in the early 20th century.

The smelter was part of the hydroelectric scheme that used the rivers cascading from

◀ The Grey Mare's Tail

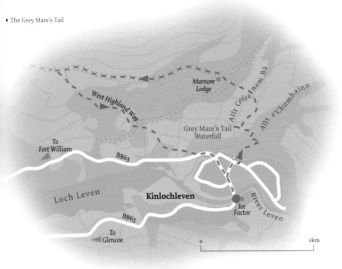

the mountains and, at its height, employed 800 people; it closed in 2000. Kinlochleven is said to have been the first village in the UK to have every house connected to electricity. It is now home to the Ice Factor, the world's biggest indoor ice-climbing wall and the National Centre for Ice Climbing, which opened in 2003 and welcomes around 150,000 visitors per year.

A rough, stony path climbs out of the oak and birch woodland onto open hillside with an outlook along the length of Loch Leven framed by stands of Scots pine and birch. The path splits here, so go left for a gradual climb over open slopes before dropping down to cross a bridge over the racing waters of the Allt Coire na Ba.

It's now a slightly tougher climb through a pocket of woodland to gain a narrow road beside what was the Mamore Lodge Hotel. Holding a stately mountainside position, this started life in the late-19th century as a shooting lodge. Turn right to pass the former hotel building and go left onto a track that climbs gradually west with easy walking and spectacular views.

After 1.5km, take the waymarked West Highland Way on the left. This winds steadily down open hillside into mixed woodland. At a fork, turn left and continue to eventually reach a road. Go straight on along the West Highland Way to the next junction. Turn right here and carry on until you meet the B863 on the outskirts of Kinlochleven. Turn left and walk back to the start.

The diversity of Lochaber's landscape is perfectly illustrated when you leave the mountainous scenery of Glencoe and Glen Nevis for the lonely and dramatic quarter of Ardgour, Moidart and the Ardnamurchan Peninsula.

Stretching west from Loch Linnhe to Ardnamurchan Point, the most westerly tip of the British mainland, this part of Lochaber is sparsely populated with its villages linked by a string of mostly single-track roads, meaning getting anywhere can take a while.

Being surrounded on three sides by water gives this region a distinctly island quality – the most popular way onto the peninsula is by the Corran Ferry over Loch Linnhe to Ardgour where five minutes on the water transports you to the much more peaceful, laid-back pace of the west shore. From the far west of Ardnamurchan, the nearest bright lights are another ferry ride away, over Loch

Sunart to the strip of shops and cafés in Tobermory on the Isle of Mull.

It's an island feel that only adds to the attraction – there are few places in Britain more alluring than here and the range of wildlife is almost without compare. The oakwoods near Strontian are one of the best places to spot wildlife, as is the stunning coastline and white sandy beaches between Portuairk at the south end of Sanna Bay and the lighthouse at Ardnamurchan Point.

The craggy slopes of Ben Hiant offer breathtaking views across much of this region as well as over to the islands of Mull, Rum and Eigg, while a lower but equally impressive vantage point can be taken in from the Crofter's Wood above Camusnagaul, a short ferry journey across Loch Linnhe from Fort William. In Moidart, the stark beauty of the landscape can be observed on a walk from Castle Tioram on Loch Moidart towards Acharacle.

Sanna Bay from Portuairk ▶

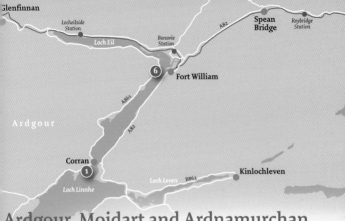

Ardgour, Moidart and Ardnamurchan

1 Corran and Clovullin round 32
Stroll along the Corran Narrows and through pleasant woodland

2 Ariundle Oakwood 34
Explore the native trees of this ancient Atlantic woodland on a walk up the Strontian River

3 Ben Hiant 36
Don't visit Ardnamurchan without heading up this characterful hill with volcanic origins and a mighty big view

4 To Ardnamurchan Lighthouse 38
Go west from Portuairk to discover the magical Bay MacNeil with an outlook to the Small Isles and marine life to spy

5 River Shiel from Castle Tioram 40
View a haunting historic ruin on an easy circuit from Loch Moidart

6 Crofter's Wood over Camusnagaul 42
Hop across Loch Linnhe from Fort William to take in one of the finest vistas in Lochaber

Corran and Clovullin round

Distance **3.5km** Time **1 hour 30**
Terrain **minor roads, tracks, roadside
verge** Map **OS Explorer 391** Access **regular
buses from Glasgow and Fort William to
Nether Lochaber; regular daily sailings
from Nether Lochaber to Corran**

The village of Ardgour sits within the
district of the same name and is the first
settlement you come to when arriving via
the short but scenic ferry route across the
Corran Narrows. Ardgour is divided
between the ferry community at Corran
and the traditional croft village of
Clovullin, which are linked by a delightful
walk of woodland and shore. The last
500m are along the verge of the A861.

From the ferry slipway, turn right onto
the A861 and pass the Inn at Ardgour,
which has served travellers since the early
19th century. The Corran Narrows (*Ceolas a
Chorrain*) has been an important crossing

point for centuries and is one of the
oldest trade routes in the Highlands.

It is only a few hundred yards wide,
but its fast-flowing waters would have
provided an anxious journey for drovers
who swam their cattle across the Narrows
on their journeys south to market.

A rowing boat was the original means
of transportation and the ferry slipway
opened in 1815, having been designed by
Scottish engineer Thomas Telford. The
first car ferry came into service in 1935 with
room for two cars. Today there are two
ferries, carrying around 250,000 vehicles
each year.

Follow the quiet road through Corran,
passing several cottages, with views to
Sgurr na h-Eanchainne ahead and Loch
Linnhe stretching away to your right. It is
thought that the name Ardgour may mean
'Promontory of the Goat' or 'Crooked
Promontory', which would certainly

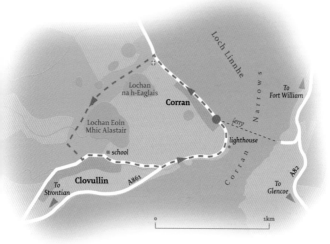

correspond to its rough, rocky topography.

After 750m, just beyond Ardgour Parish Church, turn left and go through a gate beside a cottage onto a woodland track. This proceeds southwest through broadleaf woodland which puts on a vibrant show of colour in autumn. The track runs to the right of the lovely Lochan na h-Eaglais ('the small Loch of the Church') and, soon after this, the larger Lochan Eoin Mhic Alastair. At the loch's western edge, a path leads left to the shore with views across Loch Linnhe to Beinn an Aonaich Mhor and, further south, Creag Ghorm.

Continue southwest and go straight on as a track comes in from the right. Cross an old stone bridge over a burn that feeds the second loch and then, at a junction, turn left onto a quiet, narrow road (keep an eye

out for traffic); there are views south to the angular slopes of Beinn a'Bheithir above Ballachulish.

Carry on to reach another junction at the little settlement of Clovullin. Turn left onto a minor road and continue past a few houses, Ardgour Memorial Hall and Ardgour Primary School.

This road travels east through open countryside towards Loch Linnhe and, after 500m, culminates beside the A861. Carefully cross the road (which may be busy when cars have alighted from the ferry), turn left and follow the roadside verge back towards Ardgour.

Shortly before you reach the ferry crossing, you pass Corran Lighthouse, which was built in 1860 by David and Thomas Stevenson.

◗ Sgurr na h-Enchainne from Ardgour

Ariundle Oakwood

Distance 9.5km **Time** 3 hours
Terrain minor roads, woodland and
riverside paths and tracks
Map OS Explorer 391 **Access** bus from
Fort William to Strontian

On the outskirts of Strontian, Ariundle
Oakwood is a remnant of an immense
ancient oakwood that once cloaked much
of Europe's Atlantic coast. Quiet roads
link the village with this National Nature
Reserve where good paths strike through
the woodland and alongside the Strontian
River. Located on the north shore of Loch
Sunart, the village developed during the
early 18th century as a result of silver, lead
and zinc extraction from the surrounding
landscape. Strontian means 'Promontory
of the Beacon' and gave its name to the
element Strontium which was discovered
here in 1790.

From the tourist information centre in
the heart of Strontian village, follow the
A861 across a bridge over the Strontian
River, then turn right onto a minor road
signposted for 'Ariundle Forest Walks'. This
travels easily near the river, passing several
cottages. Further along, good views open
out to the sharp peaks of Ardgour away to
the north.

After 1.5km, bear right onto a narrow
road signed for 'Aryundle' and keep on into
the 'Airigh Fhionndail National Nature
Reserve' (the Gaelic name for Ariundle)
and past the excellent Ariundle Centre,
which has a shop and restaurant. The
scenic road continues for another 750m to
a car park (an alternative start point).

Carry straight on past the car park – here
the road becomes a track which leads into
the ancient oak woodland. Other native
species found here include rowan, birch,
alder, hazel, willow and ash. During the
18th and 19th centuries the trees were
coppiced every 20 years to create wood for
charcoal burning, which was subsequently
used at the Bonawe Iron Furnace and in
Strontian Glen's lead mining industry.

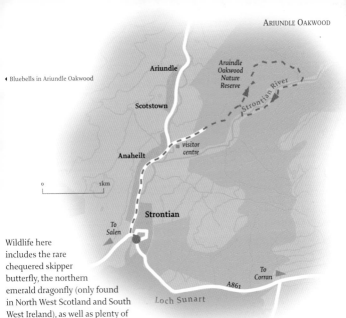

◄ Bluebells in Ariundle Oakwood

Wildlife here includes the rare chequered skipper butterfly, the northern emerald dragonfly (only found in North West Scotland and South West Ireland), as well as plenty of birdlife, such as wren, wood warbler and redstart.

After around 1km, bear left from the track onto a path signed 'Ceum Coille' (Gaelic for 'Woodland Walk'). This climbs gradually through the lichen-covered oakwoods, before a steady ascent takes you to a clearing at the top with a view of the rugged, bare hills of Ardgour – Sgurr a' Chaorainn's sharp cone is particularly prominent to the northeast. On the left stand the remains of an old croft.

A steady decent back into the woodland soon reaches a fork. Keep right to return to the main track. Go left across a footbridge, then after 20m take a waymarked path on the right.

This heads through a mix of Scots pine, birch and oak trees, crossing a section of boardwalk. At its end, the path swings right alongside the Strontian River before crossing it on a footbridge. With the water now on your right, the path continues through a lovely open glen with scattered birch and views extending along much of its length.

Walk downstream, keeping an eye out for dipper, which can only be found at the water's edge, until you reach a footbridge spanning the river. Cross this back into woodland where a path leads you to the outward track. Turn left and retrace your steps to Strontian.

35

Ben Hiant

Distance 4km **Time** 3 hours
Terrain hill paths, some steep ascents
and descents **Map** OS Explorer 390
Access bus from Fort William and
Kilchoan to Ben Hiant car park

It may only rise to 528m, but Ben Hiant
climbs steeply from a vast tract of
moorland near the western edge of
the Ardnamurchan Peninsula, making
it a prominent landmark from all
directions. Not only is this craggy peak
full of character, it also gives far-reaching
views over a magical seascape that
contains the Small Isles and the Isle of
Skye with the Outer Hebrides beyond.
A fine path climbs from the roadside to
the summit, though good navigation
skills are essential in poor visibility.
Sheep graze on the hillside, so keep
dogs on leads.

The route begins from a small car park,
adjacent to a track, on the east side of the
B8007 at its highest point. On the
opposite side of the road, there is a very
small cairn where a narrow path climbs
onto open hillside with the steep lower
flanks of Ben Hiant above.

This obvious path rises steadily and
then more steeply west, soon swinging
southwest with views stretching across
Loch Mudle and out to the distinctive
profile of the Isle of Eigg.

A more forgiving gradient takes you
beneath a craggy outcrop on the right,
after which the grassy path curves right
and continues to climb; a view along the
Sound of Mull extends south to the great
peaks of Mull rising beyond. There is also
a superb view east to Beinn Resipol and to
Ardgour's clutch of rugged mountains.

Another couple of steep pulls bring you
to a more level area where a little breather
can be enjoyed before another good

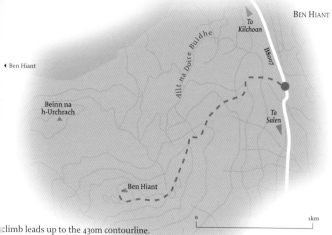

◀ Ben Hiant

climb leads up to the 430m contourline.

A series of rocky bumps now continues southwest and then west, making an exhilarating high-level walk with views sweeping north into the glen below. A stiff pull, with sharp drops to the right, leads to the steep east face of Ben Hiant – MacLean's Nose juts into the Sound of Mull to the south.

Rather than climbing up the very steep east face, the path contours left around to the south of Ben Hiant and then curves right to make a gradual ascent of its west side to the summit trig point and cairn. What initially appeared to be a tricky final push to the top is actually quite simple.

The complex geology of this corner of Ardnamurchan involves a volcanic heritage that goes back 60 million years. It attracts geologists from around the world and accounts in no small part for Lochaber's designation as a European GeoPark. Ben Hiant itself is the eroded flank of a volcano while over to the

northwest, towards the sparkling white sands of Sanna, lies the famous Ring of Ardnamurchan, the eroded crater of the ancient magma chamber that lay beneath this west of Ardnamurchan volcano.

Rum and Skye, which emerge mistily from the sea from this vantage point, are links in the same chain of volcanoes, while the Sgurr of Eigg, which gives this small isle its distinctive shape, was formed by lava erupting from Rum.

The low-lying Hebridean isles of Barra and South Uist are also visible on the horizon on a clear day. Below to the west, Kilchoan's whitewashed cottages are strung along the coast, with Ardnamurchan Lighthouse beyond.

From the summit carefully retrace your steps to the start, enjoying the views southwards across Loch Sunart to the Morvern Peninsula and the Isle of Mull and northeastwards to Moidart.

To Ardnamurchan Lighthouse

**Distance 9km Time 2 hours 30
Terrain minor roads, moorland and
coastal paths Map OS Explorer 390
Access bus from Fort William to Kilchoan,
6.5km from the start**

The Point of Ardnamurchan is the most
westerly tip of the British mainland and is
overlooked by its striking lighthouse.
The coastline here is rugged with stunted
wind-bent trees and Carribean-white
beaches peppering the rocky shore. This
picturesque adventure begins at Portuairk.

The crofting township of Portuairk faces
the curve of white sand of Sanna Bay. You
may find sheep grazing on Portuairk's own
beach, so keep dogs under strict control.

From the car park above the village, turn
right and walk downhill to the bay. Turn
left at the junction to follow the narrow
shore road past several attractive cottages.

At its end, go through two gates in quick
succession, both signed for 'Bay MacNeil'.
Glance back from here for a stunning view
across the bay to the cottages of Sanna,
while the Small Isles of Rum, Eigg and
Muck rear up from the sea. Bear left onto
a path beside a pebbly beach and pass a
cottage on your left.

The path then rises through a gully; just
beyond an old watertank after 30m, turn
right and follow the path southwest across
heathery moorland. After a marker post,
the path splits. Keep right, pass another
marker and continue over the moorland.
In a while, the path runs right of a fence
beneath the steep Sgurr nam Meann, then
descends west through a secluded glen.
Once through a gap in a wall, you come to
the remains of an old croft and a view to
Ardnamurchan Lighthouse.

To the left of the croft, cross a stile at a

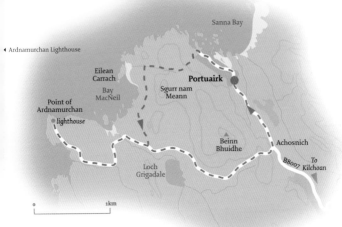

◀ Ardnamurchan Lighthouse

fence, then walk south along a path to the left of the fence. This broadens to a track and then goes through a gate into a small caravan site above the glittering sands of Bay MacNeil. This beach, with its turquoise waters and fabulous outlook, is an idyllic spot for a break.

Continue along the track through another gate, then bear left at a marker post onto a path which heads uphill, crossing a stile at a fence. Walk southeast across a rugged landscape and drop down through a gate onto the Ardnamurchan Lighthouse access road. Turn right and follow the road for the lighthouse, tearoom, shop and visitor centre.

Designed by Alan Stevenson, an uncle of Robert Louis Stevenson, the lighthouse is 36m high and built from granite quarried on Mull. It has guided ships around these treacherous waters since 1849 and is open to visitors from April to October. If the weather is on your side, don't miss the chance to climb the 152 steps and two ladders to the light room at the top. Among the islands you may see from here are Coll and Tiree, as well as the tiny uninhabited Treshnish Isles west of Mull.

It is thought that Ardnamurchan means 'Promontory of the Otters', just one of the species that you may spot; seals are another, and marine life to look out for includes harbour porpoise and bottlenose dolphin, while basking shark, minke whale and common dolphin might be seen from March to October.

Retrace your steps to pass the outward route; the road extends for a further 2km through wild scenery with rugged hills such as Ben Hiant and Beinn na Seilg to the east. Eventually the road drops down to a T-junction at Achosnich. Turn left here and return to the start.

River Shiel from Castle Tioram

Distance 4.75km **Time** 1 hour 30
Terrain beach, tracks, minor road
Map OS Explorer 390 **Access** bus from Fort
William and Kilchoan to Cul Doirlinn
road end, 3.25km from the start

Castle Tioram (pronounced 'Cheerum')
stands atop a rocky tidal island that rises
from Loch Moidart in the midst of a wild
and lonely landscape. It is the focal point
of a walk that also follows the wooded
banks of the River Shiel. Although the
castle is closed to the public, its exterior
and island can be visited at low tides –
check tide times before you set out.

The River Shiel drains the west end of
freshwater Loch Shiel by the village of
Acharacle and empties into tidal Loch
Moidart, some 5km to the north, between
the scattered estate village of Dorlin and a
headland that contains the rock-strewn
coves of Ardtoe to the east of Kentra Bay.

Cul Doirlinn car park is at the end of a
narrow road that runs for 3.25km from
the A861 at Blain. From the car park, turn
right along a narrow road by the shores
of Loch Moidart – its name translates
from Old Norse as 'Place of the Muddy
Ford' and reflects the authority the
Vikings had on Scotland's western
seaboard from the 9th to 13th centuries.
Eilean Shona, where *Peter Pan* author
J M Barrie regularly stayed in the 1920s,
lies wedged in the middle of the narrow
sea loch, across from Dorlin.

Once past Doirlinn Cottage and beyond
a gate, walk along a lovely beach to reach
a sandy causeway linking Castle Tioram
('the Dry Castle') to the mainland.

Castle Tioram commanded a strategic
location, protecting the entrance of Loch
Moidart and nearby Loch Shiel. It was
built in the 14th century after Ranald,
Chief of Clanranald, received a charter

◄ Castle Tioram

from King Robert II for his lands, which included parts of Moidart, Arisaig, Morar, Knoydart, Eigg and Rum.

Fourteen successive chiefs of Clanranald lived here until it was garrisoned by government troops in 1692 as a result of the affiliation of Allan, the 14th Chief of Clanranald, to the Jacobite cause. The garrison was taken by Allan and his men in 1715, at which point he ordered Castle Tioram to be set alight, preventing it falling back into government hands.

Retrace your steps past the car park and go round a wooden barrier, after which the road splits. Keep right onto a private road which skirts southwards above the loch, passing an old jetty and boathouse and several beautifully-situated houses.

A track then continues upstream along the River Shiel - otter, red-breasted merganser and heron are regular visitors while goldeneye may be resident during the winter. Once through a gate, the track enters mixed woodland beneath the pine-, birch- and oak-clad slopes of Torr Mor.

As the track veers left, there are views across the water to Shielfoot's scattering of houses where the remains of a vitrified fort, thought to be 2000 years old, stand.

Soon afterwards, the track passes through a white gate to meet the Cul

Doirlinn minor road. Turn left and follow this (watch for traffic) through a rugged landscape cloaked in woodland, with only the bare slopes of Beinn Gheur and Cruach nam Meann rising above the treeline. The road undulates along easily, passing the whitewashed cottage of The Square with its old phonebox, after which it drops gently back down to the car park.

Crofter's Wood over Camusnagaul

Distance 2.5km Time 1 hour
Terrain woodland and hillside paths,
minor road; a steady ascent at the start,
brief awkward section Map OS Explorer 392
Access daily passenger ferry (except
Sunday) from Fort William to
Camusnagaul or Corran Ferry from Nether
Lochaber to Ardgour and bus from
Ardgour to Camusnagaul

At the northeastern tip of the Ardgour
Peninsula just a short ferry journey across
Loch Linnhe from Fort William is
Camusnagaul. Above the loch lies the
Crofter's Wood, home to many old oak and
birch trees, mosses and lichens, and
wildflowers. The waymarked
Crofter's Trail climbs to one of the most
spectacular viewpoints in Lochaber.

Facing Loch Linnhe, at the small car park

by Camusnagaul jetty, turn left and walk
northwest along the A861, with views over
the water to Fort William and Ben Nevis.
Once through a gate by a cattle grid, turn
left onto the waymarked Crofter's Trail.

Here, a narrow path begins to climb
steadily, following white waymarks
through a woodland wonderland of sessile
oak and birch, as well as ash, rowan, alder,
beech, willow, hazel and holly. The wood is
owned and cared for by the Treslaig &
Achaphubuil Crofters Woodland Trust.

Extensive archaeological remains such as
dykes, lazy beds and hut circles have been
found here and the oak trees may have
once been coppiced for charcoal burning.

Though obvious, the path can be a little
boggy as it rises high above Loch Linnhe
through heather-clad slopes; at different
times of year, you will see bilberry,

◀ Ben Nevis across Loch Linnhe

bluebell, wood sorrel and a variety of ferns as you progress.

After going through a gate at a deer fence, turn right to follow a path which runs briefly along an old drystane dyke. It then traverses the wooded hillside with steep slopes to the right – care should be taken here.

After making its way across a couple of burns in quick succession, the path rises gradually above downy birch, swinging left onto open hillside which is home to the bright yellow flowers of bog asphodel in summer. Although this section of the route is not waymarked, the path is always clear.

Look out for an indistinct trail on the left. This leads to a bench and a stunning view across Loch Linnhe to Fort William, which seems almost insignificant against the bulk of Ben Nevis and Carn Mor Dearg. The pointed summit of Sgurr a'Mhaim is also prominent.

Return to the main path and continue for a gentle climb west along the deer fence for another 100m, before going right through a gate. Now waymarked, the path heads gradually downhill. It can be a little boggy after rain with tree roots making the descent awkward at times, but the going is

generally good with plenty of birdlife to keep you company. The path returns to the A861 after passing through a gate.

Carefully cross the road onto another waymarked path. This veers right and leads south through oak woodland and alongside Loch Linnhe to reach the A861 after about 200m. Turn left and follow the road, with more impressive views of Ben Nevis as you head all the way back to Camusnagaul.

Just like Glencoe, Glen Nevis is a walkers' paradise. Just a short distance from Fort William at the heart of the area branded 'The Outdoor Capital of the UK', the glen is dominated by Ben Nevis, the highest point in the British Isles. The popular Mountain Track (previously known – somewhat misleadingly – as the Tourist Path) offers a tough but stimulating route and a panorama worthy of its immense scale.

On the south side of Glen Nevis are the Mamores, a spectacularly rugged range of ten Munros (Scottish mountains over 3000ft). One of the most challenging routes in this guide, the monumental Ring of Steall, takes in four of these peaks in a true classic of hillwalking.

Another exhilarating walk, this time through the narrow and dramatic confines

of Steall Gorge, unexpectedly culminates at the wide-open space of Steall Meadows and the An Steall falls.

Although like Glencoe there are clearly many thrills to be found here, there are plenty of simple low-level routes in and around Fort William and Glen Nevis too.

One such walk follows the River Lochy from the town to reach the historic Inverlochy Castle, while the banks of the River Nevis also make for an attractive and peaceful walk. The Achriabhach Forest Trail further illustrates the variety of walking to be found here.

Two smaller tops, Cow Hill and Dun Deardail (home to the remains of an Iron Age fort), make great vantage points for surveying the Alpine character of this much-loved glen.

Sgurr a' Mhaim from Dun Deardail ▶

Glen Nevis

1 Inverlochy Castle by the Great Glen Way 46
History is around every corner on this short route along the River Lochy from Fort William

2 Cow Hill 48
Don't follow the herd – head up this local favourite for a great outlook

3 Along the River Nevis 50
This simple stroll is a great introduction to one of the most beautiful glens in the Highlands

4 Ben Nevis by the Mountain Track 52
Don't underestimate this hulk of a mountain – it's a challenge at any time of year and in any weather

5 Dun Deardail 54
Explore the other side of the glen from the Ben on this modest climb to an ancient hillfort

6 Achriabhach Forest 56
Further down Glen Nevis is a short but steep woodland walk which takes a different view on an Alpine landscape

7 Steall Gorge and Meadows 58
It doesn't get much better than this – ancient woodland, rocky mountains and a spectacular waterfall

8 The Ring of Steall 60
A precarious river crossing, an airy ridgewalk and four Munros make for an unforgettable day in the Mamores

Inverlochy Castle by the Great Glen Way

Distance 4.75km **Time** 1 hour 30
Terrain pavement, paths **Map** OS Explorer
392 **Access** regular trains and buses from
Glasgow to Fort William

Fort William is hailed as Scotland's
Outdoor Capital and a number of walks
begin in and around this bustling town.
One of the best leads from the town
centre to the historic Inverlochy Castle.
The return passes through the village of
Inverlochy, with its close ties to the area's
aluminium industry.

The fort that gives Fort William its name
was built in 1690 to replace the one that
had stood at Inverlochy since 1654. The
settlement was named after King William
II. During the late 19th century, the West
Highland Railway arrived and the town
expanded through the aluminium and
hydro-electricity industries.

Start from Cameron Square, outside the
excellent West Highland Museum. Facing

the pedestrianised High Street, turn right
and follow this past a number of shops
before heading down a flight of steps at
its end and continuing through an
underpass beneath the A82. Climb steps
to reach Fort William Railway Station, turn
left past its entrance and follow the Great
Glen Way sign across MacFarlane Way and
through a car park. At a roundabout, go
straight across onto Carmichael Way, then
turn right beside the fire station.

Follow this road to its end to then take
a fenced path which culminates at
Camanachd Crescent on the outskirts of
Inverlochy. Turn right and then left to
cross the bridge over the River Nevis
where it flows into Loch Linnhe, now on
Abrach Road. General Monck's Inverlochy
Fort was built here in mid-1650.

Once across, bear left at a Great Glen
waymark onto a woodland path and
follow this as it runs alongside the River
Lochy. When the path forks, keep right

◂ Inverlochy Castle

and then left at a junction.

Continue along the riverbank, after a while crossing a track. Beyond a gate, the path crosses open countryside to meet a minor road. Turn left across a bridge over a small channel and follow a minor road as it heads through an arch of a railway bridge. You are now leaving the Great Glen Way which crosses the River Lochy by a footbridge known as the Soldiers' Bridge. Ahead to your left lie the impressive remains of Inverlochy Castle. Despite its age, having been built around 1280 by the Lord of Badenoch, John Comyn, it remains in good condition.

Sited at the Great Glen's southern entrance, Inverlochy Castle was one of a number of forts that secured the Comyns as one of Scotland's most powerful families. It is associated with two major battles; in 1431 a force of Highlanders defeated a Royalist army nearby and in 1645 the Marquis of Montrose overwhelmed the Earl of Argyll's Covenanter army who were garrisoned in the castle.

Return past the point where you joined the minor road; this time stay on the road to eventually reach Locheil Road. Walk along this quiet street, passing a statue based on one of the furnace workers of the Lochaber Aluminium Smelter – it opened in 1929 and still remains a major employer in the area. The settlement was originally known as Inner Loghie, where Pictish kings resided and merchants of France and Spain bought and sold goods.

Cross Montrose Avenue onto Wades Road. This becomes Abrach Road and crosses the River Nevis. Retrace your steps into Fort William.

Cow Hill

Distance **11km** Time **3 hours**
Terrain **pavement, hill and moorland
paths** Map **OS Explorer 392** Access **bus
from Fort William to Glen Nevis Visitor
Centre from Tuesday to Sunday**

Rising to 287m above Fort William and
Glen Nevis, Cow Hill is dwarfed by its
bigger mountain neighbours. However,
despite its lowly stature it gives some of
the best views of Ben Nevis, the Mamores
and Loch Linnhe. Good paths make their
way through woods and across moorland
to gain the top.

From Glen Nevis Visitor Centre (there is
a charge if you are leaving your car for
more than an hour), turn left onto the
Glen Nevis road, follow the pavement for
roughly 100m, then take a path on the
right signposted for the West Highland
Way. This leads past a small cemetery and
into woodland, where it climbs steadily
to a track.

Go straight across this onto the Peat
Track, leaving the West Highland Way for
a steep, prolonged ascent through larch
and spruce woodland scattered with
beech, birch and rowan. The path is good,
with views back to Meall an t-Suidhe and
Ben Nevis providing a good excuse for a
breather. The gradient finally relents as
the path emerges onto open hillside,

having gained about 50m in height.

Just before a gate, turn right onto the Cow Hill Link. A path descends gently into peaceful woodland high above Glen Nevis and traverses the lower eastern slopes of Cow Hill. It soon runs through a clearing with magnificent views along the glen before re-entering the trees and continuing for around a km to a junction.

Turn left to bear west to a viewpoint with a vista sweeping across Fort William and Loch Linnhe. After another few metres, go left again for a gradual climb with views opening out along Loch Linnhe to the Ardgour hills of Meall an t-Slamain and Meall Ruadh.

Keep along the path as it bears southwest to reach a fork. Take the left branch to continue across open hillside, home to careering swift and wheatear in summer and flamboyant flight displays by buzzards in spring. Where the route splits again, keep left and follow a long straight path to reach a gate.

Once through, go left onto a stony track which climbs steadily southeast and then

east, with the long ridge of Bidhein Bad na h-Iolaire and then the high slopes of Ben Nevis dominating the view. At a fork at the top of the track, bear left and continue towards the summit of Cow Hill.

Once over a stile beside a gate, the track drops before climbing north to the top where the panorama extends southeast along Glen Nevis to Sgurr a' Mhaim and Stob Ban in the Mamores range and northwest to Corpach, the Narrows and Loch Eil beyond.

Retrace your steps over the stile to where the path splits. Turn left to continue down through a gate and soon pick up the outward path. Carry straight on and walk back down to the start.

◄ Glen Nevis from Cow Hill

Along the River Nevis

Distance 4.5km **Time** 1 hour 30
Terrain pavement, riverside and
woodland paths **Map** OS Explorer 392
Access bus from Fort William to
**Glen Nevis Visitor Centre from Tuesday
to Sunday**

**The clear waters of the River Nevis are the
focal point of this walk that meanders
along its banks with a return through
woodland on the west side of Glen Nevis.
There are fine views of the mountains
that dominate the head of the glen.**

The Glen Nevis Visitor Centre is open
throughout the year and provides lots of
information about Ben Nevis and the
surrounding landscape, its flora and
fauna. There is a charge for the car park if
you are leaving your car for more than
one hour.

From the visitor centre, follow the

riverside path north through the car park
to reach a wooden suspension bridge over
the River Nevis.

Once across, turn right and follow a
pleasant though sometimes boggy path
south alongside the fast-flowing river.
The path hugs the eastern bank with the
steep slopes of Meall an t-Suidhe rising to
the left. It soon passes Achintee Farm and
then a path on the left for Ben Nevis,
whose huge girth makes it a constant
companion on this outward section
of the route.

Walk straight on for the youth hostel,
keeping an eye out for sandpiper, dipper
and pied wagtail, with views along the
length of Glen Nevis to the lofty peaks of
Sgurr a' Mhaim and Stob Ban.

Several footbridges are crossed along
the way. When you reach a bridge over the
river, turn right across it to meet the Glen

◀ Glen Nevis

Nevis road beside Glen Nevis Youth Hostel. Turn right and follow the pavement for a few hundred metres. Once past the Glen Nevis Restaurant, turn left at a West Highland Way sign and follow a minor road through Glen Nevis Estates with views south to Sgorr Chalum and southwest to Bidhein Bad na h-Iolaire.

The road climbs steadily past a few cottages onto a forested track. Beyond a gate, you continue to a T-junction where you turn right to follow a wide track north through the forest. When the West Highland Way comes in from the left, carry straight on and drop downhill to reach a four-way marker post.

Bear right here onto a beautiful little woodland path, which winds its way downhill, exiting the wood through a gap in a wall. The path passes a small cemetery on your left and proceeds through open countryside back to the Glen Nevis road. Turn left and return to the Glen Nevis Visitor Centre.

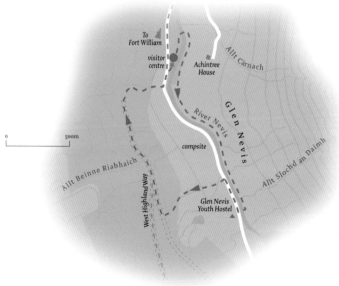

Ben Nevis by the Mountain Track

Distance **17km** Time **8 hours**
Terrain **mountain paths with some steep
ascents/descents** Maps **OS Explorer 392**
Access **bus from Fort William to Glen
Nevis Visitor Centre from Tuesday
to Sunday**

At 1344m, the summit of Ben Nevis is
the highest point in the British Isles.
Around 125,000 walkers reach the summit
annually with most ascents made via the
Mountain Track. Although this is the
simplest means of reaching the top it is
still a very challenging route, even on
a clear summer's day, with more than
1340m to climb (and descend). Ben Nevis
must never be underestimated, especially
in poor visibility or winter conditions –
snow on or near the summit may last
well into the summer. You should wear
proper hillwalking attire at any time
of year.

From the Glen Nevis Visitor Centre car
park (there is a charge if leaving your car
for more than one hour), follow the
riverside path north and cross the wooden
suspension bridge over the River Nevis.
Turn right and then, beyond Achintee
Farm, turn left onto a path for Ben Nevis.

This climbs to a stile. Once over, cross a
track, then turn right onto the Mountain
Track, which was built in 1883 as an access
route for the summit observatory.
A gradual climb leads southeast above
Glen Nevis with views over to Stob Ban.

After 1km, a path from the youth hostel
comes in from the right. Carry straight on
and continue up the path, which is quite
bouldery in places. Soon after crossing a
large wooden footbridge the path swings
left and a breathtaking view of Ben Nevis
opens up. The path rises northeast above
the gushing waters of the Allt na h-
Urchaire ('the Red Burn'), soon making

◂ On the summit of Ben Nevis

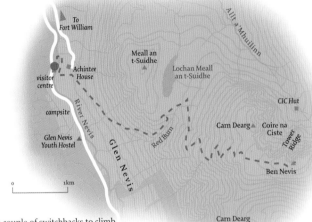

a couple of switchbacks to climb above Lochan Meall an t'Suidhe, often known as the Halfway Lochan. Don't be fooled though – the real halfway point is a little higher up.

At a junction, turn right and continue to climb, enjoying views of the Mamores. Cross the Allt na h-Urchaire, the true halfway point of ascent – this is also the last watersource so it's a good idea to fill up waterbottles.

Upon reaching a height of 750m, a series of zigzags begins. This is a tougher section, rougher underfoot with a steepening gradient, though it is not without its rewards – the views west along Loch Eil and southwest to Ardgour and Glencoe are outstanding.

Now, the winding path rises to 1200m. From here, pay special attention to sticking to it as it climbs steadily east – the path is lined with marker cairns and real care must be taken in poor visibility to avoid the vertiginous cliffs of Coire na Ciste plunging some 700m into the glen below.

You soon gain the sprawling, barren summit plateau and now Ben Nevis' grandeur can truly be appreciated, particularly that of the North Face. On a clear day Schiehallion, Skye's Cuillin Ridge and the Paps of Jura can all be seen. The remains of the observatory are also visible. Clement Wragge first recorded meteorological data on Ben Nevis in 1881 and the observatory was open between 1883 and 1904. The building, instruments and meteorologists withstood some of Scotland's severest weather conditions.

From the summit, retrace your steps to Achintee with views all the way.

Dun Deardail

**Distance 9.5km Time 2 hours 30
Terrain pavement, woodland and hillside
paths; sustained ascent Map OS Explorer
392 Access bus from Fort William to
Glen Nevis Visitor Centre from Tuesday
to Sunday**

The West Highland Way climbs above
Glen Nevis to reach the base of Dun
Deardail (pronounced 'Dun Jee-ard All').
From here, a short climb along a good
path tackles its summit, one that was
once a fort and a perfect vantage point to
survey much of Glen Nevis and the
surrounding mountains.

Begin from the Glen Nevis Visitor
Centre where there is a large car park
(there is a charge if you are leaving your
car for more than one hour).

Turn left onto the Glen Nevis road and

follow the pavement for roughly 100m,
then take a path on the right signposted
for the West Highland Way. This leads
past a small cemetery and into woodland
to climb steadily to a track.

Turn left (waymarked for Dun Deardail)
and walk south along the wide forestry
track of the West Highland Way. It rises
gently through attractive mixed woodland
with the distinctive outline of Sgurr a'
Mhaim ahead while the steep slopes of
Beinn Riabhach rise to the right. Many of
the approaching walkers will be weary
ones, as they are near the end of their
West Highland Way journey, having
walked most of the 154km (as well as
climbed more than 4500m) from
Milngavie on the outskirts of Glasgow to
Fort William.

After nearly 1.25km, the track splits.

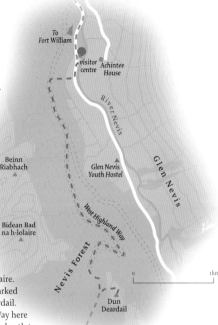

◀ Ben Nevis from Dun Deardail

Take the right branch for a prolonged and steady ascent rising high above Glen Nevis. A good walking rhythm can be found and if a break is required the views of Ben Nevis are superb. The top of Dun Deardail can be seen poking its head above the trees to the south.

After a while, the track levels off and enters dense larch woodland, although the steady climb soon begins again. In turn, a series of zigzags wind uphill with views of Bidean Bad na h-Iolaire. Eventually you gain a waymarked path on the left for Dun Deardail.

Leave the West Highland Way here and follow the excellent gravel path to the left of a conifer plantation. It soon curves right and climbs steeply over grassy slopes towards the summit. The final ascent is on a path with a series of steps which arcs left onto Dun Deardail.

The top still holds the visible remains of the fort that was built around 2000 years ago and occupied for various periods of time over the centuries. It is unclear when people last lived here, but it is certain that the fort was destroyed by fire, having been deliberately set alight, with the intense heat melting the rock, a process known as vitrification.

From the turf-covered walls, the view extends across Glen Nevis and the river to the flanks of Ben Nevis and then south to the shapely slopes of Sgurr a' Mhaim and Stob Ban. Loch Linnhe and Fort William are also clearly visible to the north. Once you've soaked up the views, rejoin the West Highland Way and its weary troop of long-distance walkers and then retrace your steps to the visitor centre.

Achriabhach Forest

Distance 3.5km **Time** 1 hour
Terrain woodland paths and tracks; one
steep climb **Map** OS Explorer 392
Access bus from Fort William to
Achriabhach from Tuesday to Sunday

Although this walk is short, it contains
one long, steep ascent that gets the legs
and lungs working. The pay-off is a
sweeping perspective over Glen Nevis and
the mountains that envelop it on all sides.

The route starts from the Lower Falls car
park, a few miles along the Glen Nevis road
from Fort William. Before beginning the
walk, it is worth the short detour down
to Lower Falls Bridge over the River Nevis
to see the dramatic waterfalls.

Retrace your steps along the Glen Nevis
road past the car park and drop west across
a bridge over the Allt a' Choire Dheirg.
This river, which translates from Gaelic
as 'Stream of the Red Corrie', is followed
for a good part of the walk.

After passing the lovely whitewashed
Achriabhach Cottage, take a track on the
left (if arriving by bus alight here), but just
as you enter Achriabhach Forest turn left
onto a path which then climbs along the

left edge of woodland and to the right of the Allt a' Choire Dheirg.

Once over a stile continue to climb steadily southwest, enjoying the sight of waterfalls cascading down into the glen as you go. The path gets steeper, although the waterfalls and birdlife provide plenty of excuses for a break.

The sustained ascent at last brings you to a wide forestry track, with the shapely outline of Stob Ban rising ahead. Two tracks go off to the right, but ignore these and take the path directly ahead.

This again rises sharply through mixed woodland, soon reaching a viewpoint to the left of the path. Here, the river has smoothed the rock into a chute, while looking along Glen Nevis several of the bulky Munros of the Mamores, including An Gearanach, vie for attention. The tight confines of the glen, the high mountains and the pockets of woodland give the scene an alpine quality. Keep an eye out for buzzard and raven utilising the thermals above.

After around 137m of ascent from Glen Nevis, the path eventually gains another forestry track. Turn right onto this and descend, with fine views north along Glen Nevis and over to Ben Nevis. The path

enters pine woodland and continues to drop down to a junction.

Go right and walk gently downhill, with the spectacle of Sgurr a' Mhaim ahead, to reach the junction of paths at the outward route. The track turns left here and descends northwest for 500m to another turning. Go right and walk down to a gate.

Once through this, continue back to the Glen Nevis road, head right and retrace your steps to the car park.

◀ Glen Nevis from Achriabhach

Steall Gorge and Meadows

Distance **3km** Time **1 hour 30**
Terrain **woodland paths – narrow and
exposed on some sections**
Map **OS Explorer 392** Access **no public
transport to the start**

Rightly hailed as one of the best short
walks in Scotland, the tight confines of
Steall Gorge guarantee thrills and drama
along its length, with the picturesque
open scenery of Steall Meadows and the
impressive backdrop of An Steall waterfall
a fitting finalé. Care should be taken
throughout, as several sections of the
path through Steall Gorge can be rocky
and slippery with steep drops below.

Start from the car park at the end of the
public road in Glen Nevis. Take the path at
the end of the car park, pausing to view the
Allt Coire Eoghainn plunging some 350m
down the steep southern slopes of Ben
Nevis into the River Nevis. The path leads
you east, with the steep slopes of Meall
Cumhann rising craggily ahead as it climbs
gradually through birch woodland above
the gorge, waterfalls cascading down
below you.

In a while, a rocky section of path crosses
a waterfall. Surrounded by steep-sided
mountains, the dramatic and picturesque
Steall Gorge is cared for by the John Muir
Trust, the charity dedicated to protecting

Meall
Cumhann

Glen Nevis

Blàr
Bàn

Water of Nevis

Steall Gorge

Càthar
na Seilge

An Steall
(waterfall)

Allt an t-Snaig

Creag nan
Eun

0   500m

wild places like this. Ancient woodland, including stands of alder, ash, birch, elm, aspen and Scots pine, cloak the slopes.

The drops get steeper down to the right and several more waterfalls tumble down the hillside into the gorge below. The path soon narrows, but if care is taken then few problems are encountered. However, if the path is wet or icy then you need to be more cautious.

Further on, there are views west along the glen into the scoured bowl of Coire Riabhach beneath Mullach nan Coirean. A rocky section drops down over another burn with a short climb up steps, then over a bridge. From here, continue just above the river, where whitewater has smoothed and eroded the rock over many millennia into amazing shapes.

Soon afterwards, the path emerges into the alpine glen of Steall Meadows. After the confines of the wooded gorge, the open space of the meadow is even more unexpected.

Rearing above the head of the meadow is the Munro peak of An Gearanach from which the magnificent An Steall ('The White Spout') plummets 120m into the river below – it is Britain's second highest waterfall. The meadow is a wonderful place to linger with the silence only really broken by the sound of An Steall.

If you wish, you can carry on along the path past the wire bridge to reach the old ruins at Steall, which date from the 1700s and were used by shepherds up until the 1940s.

Carefully retrace your steps to the car park, enjoying the fine views of the glen and Ben Nevis.

◀ Steall Meadows

The Ring of Steall

Distance 15km Time 8 hours
Terrain hill paths; several steep ascents
and descents; navigation skills required
Map OS Explorer 392 Access no public
transport to the start

The Ring of Steall is one of Scotland's
classic mountain walks. Although there
are good paths, it takes in four Munros
with three additional tops over 3000ft,
as well as the narrow Devil's Ridge
– it is a big day out that should not be
underestimated. In poor weather, good
navigation skills are essential and in
winter the Ring of Steall is a very serious
undertaking. It is best attempted on a
clear summer's day, with attention given
to hours of daylight remaining.

From the car park, take the path that
climbs through the woodland high above
the dramatic Steall Gorge. This can be
uneven with drops, so take care. After
around 1km, the path emerges into the
beautiful Steall Meadows. Continue
towards the spectacular An Steall waterfall
then bear right to follow a narrower path
to a three-wire bridge over the River Nevis.

Once across, turn left through a pocket of
woodland, passing Steall Hut, and cross
two burns. At the foot of An Gearanach
turn right and climb a very steep path
south. This zigzags through the rocky
slopes to gain its 982m summit, the first
Munro of the day with rewarding views
across the glen to Ben Nevis.

From the summit, continue south along
the narrow ridge over An Garbhanach.
A steep descent and then stiff ascent to

Meall
Cumhan

To
Fort William

Glen Nevis

Water of Nevis

waterfall

An
Gearanach

An
Garbhanach

Sgùrr
a'Mhaim

Stob Coire
a'Chairn

0   2km

The Mamores

Stob Ban

Sgùrr
an Iubhair

Am Bodach

Stob Coire
na h-Eirghe

Sgùrr an
Fhuarain

regain the height lost leads up to the cairn on the second Munro of Stob Coire a'Chairn. Its central position within the Mamores range allows for great views east to Binnein Mor and Binnein Beag.

The gradient eases slightly as the route descends southwest to reach the base of Am Bodach, the third Munro. However, a thigh-burning climb southwest up a rocky path is required to reach its lofty summit with a commanding view which extends to the Paps of Jura on a clear day.

Descend west to a narrow bealach and climb onto the summit of Sgùrr an Iubhair. The trickiest part of the route now begins. The path descends northwest to another bealach. It then heads north over the short but very narrow and exposed Devil's Ridge, which, depending on your head for heights, might be painless or may demand all your nerve. If so, a slightly less

exposed path descends left from the ridge, though either route requires extreme care.

Once the ridge is behind you, wide, quartzite slopes rise easily onto Sgùrr a' Mhaim, the highest, fourth and final Munro of the day with great views of Stob Ban, Mullach nan Coirean and the mountains of Glencoe.

A path now zigzags northwest down an obvious ridge. After a physically and mentally demanding day, you may be drained, so time should be taken on this descent. Continue down into Glen Nevis to reach a path beside the Allt Coire a' Mhusgain. Bear right and follow this down to the Glen Nevis road at Achriabhach. Turn right and walk along the road over the Lower Falls Bridge. From here, it is 2.5km back to the start.

◀ Sgùrr a'Mhaim and the Devil's Ridge

61

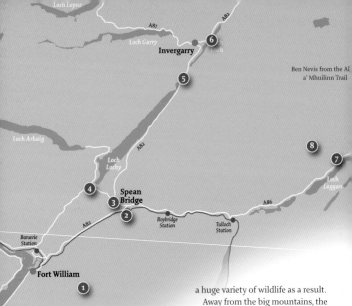

Ben Nevis from the Al a' Mhuilinn Trail

For all its immense proportions Ben Nevis is actually quite a retiring peak, its 700m-high cliffs hidden from view from most vantage points by its vast mountain slopes. However, by following the course of the Allt a' Mhuilinn to reach the Charles Inglis Clark Memorial Hut, its sheer scale and grandeur comes to the fore and it becomes clear why Ben Nevis is so attractive to geologists and climbers.

Northeast of Ben Nevis above Loch Laggan, Creag Meagaidh – and more specifically the amphitheatre of Coire Ardair – is also celebrated for its cliffs. Creag Meagaidh National Nature Reserve contains one of Scotland's most diverse range of habitats, from ancient alder woodland to arctic plateau and is home to a huge variety of wildlife as a result.

Away from the big mountains, the geology of Lochaber is equally fascinating, chiefly along the Great Glen Fault, where the freshwater Lochs Oich and Lochy are the focal points of both simple and challenging walks, utilising woodland paths and the towpath of the Caledonian Canal, a modern-day engineering marvel.

The village of Spean Bridge makes an ideal central base to explore the landscape featured in this chapter, with a couple of excellent walks right on its doorstep. Spean Bridge is also home to one of Scotland's most recognisable and much-loved landmarks, the Commando Memorial, which stands sentinel above the village. Nearby is High Bridge, thought to be the point where the first shots of the Jacobite Uprising of 1745 were fired.

Spean Bridge

1 The North Face of Ben Nevis 64
There's no summit cairn to claim, but this really is the best view of the highest peak in the British Isles

2 Killiechonate Woodlands 66
Weave through the forest on easy trails, looking out for the birdlife and fine mountain views

3 Commando Memorial and Highbridge 68
An iconic sculpture in a ruggedly majestic setting and a site with a role in Jacobite history are the highlights of this tour

4 The Moy Bridge from Gairlochy 70
Visit a lighthouse by Loch Lochy, then follow the Caledonian Canal on a minor road and towpath

5 Laggan Locks and the Caledonian Canal 72
Walk along the canal towpath and the Great Glen Way before returning to the Locks by the old railway line

6 Loch Oich loop 74
Circumnavigate the little sister of Lochs Lochy and Ness on forest tracks and good shoreline paths

7 Creag Meagaidh Nature Reserve 76
Explore the varied habitat, and its wildlife, that lies in the shadow of a mighty mountain massif

8 Coire Ardair 78
A memorable route through wild scenery leads to an atmospheric lochan at the foot of Creag Meagaidh's huge cliffs

The North Face of Ben Nevis

Distance 11km **Time** 4 hours
Terrain woodland and hill paths with
some steep ascents/descents
Map OS Explorer 392 **Access** buses from
Fort William and Inverness to Torlundy
road end, a short walk from the start

Although the objective of this walk is the
Charles Inglis Clark (CIC) Memorial Hut,
the focal point is the breathtaking view
of the north face of Ben Nevis, not visible
to walkers who tackle the Ben by the
Mountain Track. The hut sits at 680m
above sea level, meaning snow and ice
may line the upper reaches of the route
from late autumn well into spring.

The North Face car park is 1km
southeast of the A82 at Torlundy. From
here, turn left onto a wide forestry track
signposted for the Allt a' Mhuilinn and

Ben Nevis North Face, cross a bridge over
the Allt na Caillich and go round a barrier.
When the track sweeps left, turn right
onto a waymarked path for a stiff,
sustained climb through woodland.

Where the path forks, keep right and
continue to ascend. After around 750m,
you reach a viewpoint beside a bench
with an outlook towards Ben Nevis' North
Face. Shortly afterwards, the path splits.

Go right, above birch-clad slopes,
climbing past a picnic bench with views of
Loch Linnhe. At a junction, carry straight
on alongside the Allt 'a Mhuilinn and at
the next junction go right.

Beyond a stile by a gate, a good path
rises gradually southeast over open
hillside with the outlook dominated by
Ben Nevis and Carn Mor Dearg, linked by
the exposed Carn Mor Dearg Arête.

The CIC Hut

To Spean Bridge
Torlundy
A82
Allt a'Mhuilinn car park
To Fort William
Allt Coire an Lochain
Allt a' Mhuilinn
Carn Beag Dearg
Meall an t-Suidhe
Lochan Meall an t-Suidhe
Carn Mòr Dearg
CIC Hut
Carn Dearg
Tower Ridge
Ben Nevis

0   1km

The glen narrows as the path makes its way beneath Carn Mor Dearg and the enormous cliffs of Ben Nevis' northern aspect. Stepping stones cross a number of tributary burns and the walking is a delight. In time the ascent steepens, although steps at various points make the going easier. As you approach the CIC Hut, the Allt a' Mhuilinn drops in a series of waterfalls where shelves of rock have been smoothed by the raging waters.

Just before the hut, the path becomes a little rougher. Climb carefully on the last section to reach the hut, which sits on the river's south bank, although this is not difficult to cross.

The hut was built in 1928-29 by William and Jane Inglis Clark as a memorial to their son, Charles, who was killed in action during the First World War. Extensive refurbishment of the CIC Hut took place between 2008 and 2012, and it comprises accommodation for 24 people, with six places reserved at weekends during winter for members of the Scottish Mountaineering Club.

Its location is hard to beat, surrounded by one of the finest landscapes in Lochaber with the colossal buttresses of Coire Leis and Carn Dearg rising skywards for several hundred metres.

The return journey drops back along the route of ascent with a sweeping view down the glen.

Killiechonate Woodlands

Distance 4.5km **Time** 1 hour 30
Terrain minor road, woodland paths and
tracks **Map** OS Explorer 392 **Access** regular
trains from Glasgow and Fort William and
buses from Fort William and Inverness to
Spean Bridge

Killiechonate Woodlands lie to the south
of Spean Bridge and the River Spean with
a number of waymarked trails offering
great walks. This figure-of-eight route
makes its way through tranquil mixed
woodland with an assortment of wildlife
and plenty of good views.

The 'bridge' in Spean Bridge refers to
Highbridge which spans the River Spean a
little west of the village. The derivation of
'Spean' is unclear, but may come from the
Brythonic for 'hawthorn' or from the Celtic
squeas, meaning 'vomit' or 'gush'.

From the railway station, walk down
Station Road to a junction and turn right.
Follow the road past a number of houses
and alongside the fast-flowing River Spean
to cross a railway bridge after 500m.

Ahead is a small car park. Turn right just
before it onto a gated stony track for a
steady ascent into Killiechonate Woodland.
The British Aluminium Company
purchased what was open moorland in the
1920s and subsequently planted the trees
between the 1950s and 1970s. It comprises
mainly conifer species mixed with native
broadleaf and pine.

Where the track sweeps left and then
right to a junction, take the signposted
'Circular Path' ahead. This runs initially
alongside the forest track before veering
away to the left. Keep an eye out for
treecreeper, great spotted woodpecker and

◄ Glen Spean

song thrush, as well as roe deer, as the path rises gently to a junction.

Go left onto the 'Spean Bridge Circular Path' to follow a forestry track east. The conifers soon thin, with views of the Grey Corries opening out. Keep on past a bench for around 15m, then turn left at a wooden post and cross a footbridge. A lovely little path descends easily through conifer woodland, crossing another footbridge to regain the forestry track.

Go left to follow the track, with views across Glen Spean to the mountains bounding Loch Laggan, the source of the River Spean.

The track soon swings left and continues

its descent but, when it then bears right just before a minor road, go left onto a path. This meanders its way west through oak woodland, eventually returning to the outward path beside the first 'Circular Path' sign.

Turn left and follow the forestry track for around 50m before taking a narrow path on the right for Spean Bridge Station. A gradual descent through picturesque woodland soon emerges at a car park beside the railway station and Spean Bridge Golf Course. Turn right and cross a railway bridge, passing the old station building which is now a restaurant, to return to Station Road.

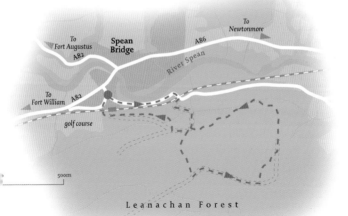

Commando Memorial and Highbridge

Distance **5.5km** Time **2 hours**
Terrain **pavement, woodland and
riverside paths** Map **OS Explorer 399**
Access **regular trains from Glasgow and
Fort William and buses from Fort William
and Inverness to Spean Bridge**

The Commando Memorial above Spean
Bridge is one of the most recognisable
landmarks in Lochaber and it presents a
thought-provoking focal point to this
walk. The route also visits Highbridge,
believed to be the point where the first
shots of the Jacobite Uprising of 1745
were fired. Livestock may be grazing on
the moorland and within the woods, so
dogs must be kept on leads here.

From the railway station follow Station
Road all the way round to the A82, then
turn right and walk through Spean Bridge.
Once across the River Spean, the road

swings left and climbs steadily for just
over 1.5km. Just before the Commando
Memorial, the pavement veers left away
from the A82 and continues along an old
road, passing the iconic 5m-high
memorial, which was unveiled in 1952.

It commemorates the elite Second
World War commandos who took part in
military exercises a few miles away at
Achnacarry Training Centre, with only the
best going on to wear the illustrious
Green Beret. From the memorial are
sweeping views of the Grey Corries, the
Aonachs and Ben Nevis.

Before reaching the B8004, turn left
through a wooden gate signposted 'Spean
Bridge via Historic High Bridge' onto a
path that runs across moorland, initially
parallel with the B-road. After this, it
sweeps left and drops down to cross a
footbridge over a burn.

◀ The Commando Memorial

Shortly after entering some woodland, the path swings sharp left. Beyond a couple of footbridges, it descends to pick up the line of the old railway where an easy section of the walk now heads southeast with views down into the River Spean Gorge where the remains of High Bridge lie.

Standing at more than 24m high, it cost £1087 when built in 1736 and is the highest of 40 bridges constructed along the 400km of General Wade's military road. The bridge formed an important link between the garrisons of Fort William, Fort Augustus and Inverness and was where the Highbridge Skirmish took place, the first dispute of the Jacobite Uprising of 1745.

Carry on along the path which, in a while, bears left from the railway line and drops down to cross a footbridge beside the remains of an old viaduct that took the Invergarry and Fort Augustus Railway across the River Spean. Continue east along a beautiful section of the River Spean, crossing several footbridges along the way. There is one short steep ascent.

As Spean Bridge is approached, you'll see Kilmonivaig Church, which dates from the 18th century, up to the left. It is named after Saint Naomhag, who was Abbot of Lismore in the 6th century. Soon afterwards, pass through a gate to regain the A82. Turn right and walk downhill into Spean Bridge.

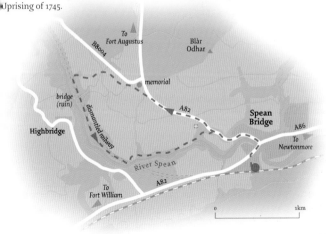

The Moy Bridge from Gairlochy

Distance 6km Time 2 hours
Terrain minor road, canal towpath
Map OS Explorer 399 Access regular buses
from Fort William to Gairlochy

This easy walk takes a quiet road from Gairlochy and drops down to the lovely Moy Bridge on the Caledonian Canal, returning by the towpath, with a short detour to Loch Lochy at the start and spectacular scenery throughout.

Gairlochy consists of a scattering of houses beside the Caledonian Canal. Building of the canal began in the early 1800s to provide safe passage for ships travelling between the North Sea and the Atlantic coast, negating the need for the arduous journey through the Pentland Firth and around Cape Wrath.

It was designed by Thomas Telford (who oversaw progress at Gairlochy from the Lockkeeper's Cottage), following

survey work by James Watt, and opened in 1822 with further construction work taking place between 1843 and 1847. It runs for 96km between Corpach on tidal Loch Linnhe and Inverness, with two-thirds of the journey along Lochs Lochy, Oich and Ness. Originally Gairlochy only had one lock – the upper lock was added in 1844 when floods submerged surrounding farmland.

The walk begins from the south side of Gairlochy Swing Bridge. Do not cross the bridge; instead turn right through a gate and walk northeast along the canal towpath and past the Gairlochy Top Lock. Continue past a basin where many boats are moored, with views of the Grey Corries to the southeast.

Beyond two gates, a grassy path culminates at the southern edge of Loch Lochy beside a distinctive little pepperpot lighthouse with views along the loch.

◄ Caledonian Canal at Gairlochy

Retrace your steps to Gairlochy, cross the Caledonian Canal by the Swing Bridge and follow the B8004 for Banavie and Fort William. This rises gradually above the canal; at the top of the climb, bear left over a bridge with an outlook across the canal and the River Lochy to Ben Nevis. Carry on along the road as it descends easily southwest for 1.25km to Moy Farm.

Turn left onto the access road (this is a working farm so keep dogs on leads); just before several buildings, turn right through a gate onto a track which sweeps left and then right alongside the canal to Moy Bridge. This is a beautiful spot to take in the surrounding landscape. The distinctive cast-iron bridge was constructed in North Wales before being assembled here in 1821 and is the only original bridge along the canal. Even

today the lockkeeper has to open the south gate first before rowing across to open the second gate.

Cross Moy Bridge (although if it is already open you may have to wait some time), turn left and walk northeast along an idyllic section of the towpath. Further on, it slips between the still waters of the canal and the less sedate River Lochy, where you may find yourself in the company of buzzards, siskin and grey heron. The towpath extends for 1.5km back to Gairlochy.

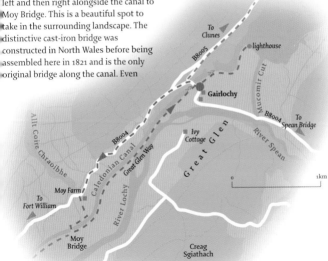

Laggan Locks and the Caledonian Canal

Distance 6.5km **Time** 2 hours
Terrain canal towpath, paths
Map OS Explorer 400 **Access** regular
buses from Glasgow, Fort William and
Inverness to Laggan Locks

A scenic section of the Caledonian Canal
links Lochs Lochy and Oich with a towpath
making a straightforward waterside stroll.
The return journey is along a dismantled
old railway line, with more easy walking
through fine countryside.

The walk begins from Laggan Locks
public car park just off the A82. Coming
out of the car park onto the access road,
turn left to cross a bridge and go through
another small car park to reach the
Caledonian Canal, with a view that extends
along Loch Lochy. It was near here that the
curiously named Battle of the Shirts was
contested in 1544 between the combined

clan forces of the Frasers and Grants and
the Camerons and Donalds. It is said that
as the day of the battle was so hot both
sides tossed aside their plaids and fought
in their shirts.

Don't cross the canal, but turn right just
before a lock and follow the towpath with
the canal to your left. This, at 32m, is the
highest point of the Caledonian Canal and
consequently the construction of Laggan
Locks was a massive undertaking with
enormous amounts of earth dug out by
250 workmen. The canal was officially
opened in 1822.

The flat towpath (part of the Great Glen
Way) makes for easy walking as it heads
northeast into woodland, with the canal
reflecting the trees where red squirrels
make their home. Pine forest soon gives
way to mixed woodland and in due course
you reach a fork beside a house and a sign

◀ Loch Lochy

for the Great Glen Way Hostel.

Bear left and cross a wooden footbridge over a burn. The trees are left behind as the towpath runs between the canal and the A82 with views opening out over steep wooded hills. When the path splits, keep left and continue until it ends beside the A82, just before Laggan Swing Bridge and Loch Oich.

Go straight across the bridge onto a side road signposted for the Great Glen Water Park. Once past the entrance to this holiday park and just before a 'No Entry' sign, turn right onto a track which leads to what was once Invergarry Railway Station. Here, turn right onto the old Spean Bridge to Fort Augustus Railway Line, built between 1896 and 1903. It ceased taking passengers in 1933, but freight traffic continued until 1947.

A path, which can be boggy at times, runs southwest with steep wooded slopes rising to the left and several impressive

waterfalls tumbling down the hillside. Carry on until you gain a wide forestry track. Go straight on, eventually passing a little cottage that sits below to the right. At this point, keep an eye out for a narrow path that peels away from the track to the right. Follow this for a gradual descent through trees to the A82. Carefully cross here, turning right and then left back onto the Laggan Locks access road. Return to the start.

Map labels:
To Fort Augustus
Loch Oich
Laggan Swing Bridge
activity centre
North Laggan
Caledonian Canal
Great Glen Way
A82
Great Glen
South Laggan
Laggan Locks
Ceann Loch
To Fort William
0   1km

Loch Oich loop

Distance 17km **Time** 4 hours
Terrain **forest and lochside paths and**
tracks; short section of roadside verge
Map OS Explorer 400 **Access** **regular**
buses from Fort William and Inverness
to Invergarry

Loch Oich sits between the larger Lochs
Lochy and Ness, and all three are linked
by the Caledonian Canal. Forest tracks
climb high above Loch Oich's northern
fringes while a good path runs along the
length of its southern shore, making for
a long and tough but rewarding walk.

Facing Invergarry Post Office on the A87
through the village, take the path to the
right of the building, signposted for
Tomdoun. There is a small car park here.

Walk downhill to cross the River Garry
via a suspension bridge, pass through a
gate and turn right. After another gate, go
left along the edge of a field onto a path
which climbs to a minor road. Turn left
here, cross a cattle grid and then

immediately bear right onto a forestry
track which is part of the Great Glen Way.
This rises gradually east through pleasant
mixed woodland.

In a while, the track curves south. When
a track joins from the right, keep straight
on to reach the walk's highest point
beside a picnic bench with a view north
along Loch Oich and the Great Glen. The
track now heads southwest. When it forks
keep left, dropping gently for 1.5km to the
A82, just north of Laggan Swing Bridge.

Turn right, following a paved path and
then a short section of roadside verge to
cross the Caledonian Canal as it enters
Loch Oich. Here, turn left onto a side road
for the Great Glen Water Park. Pass the
entrance to this holiday park and then
just before a 'No Entry' sign, turn right
and follow a track to what was once
Invergarry Railway Station.

Here, turn left onto the old Spean
Bridge to Fort Augustus Railway Line and

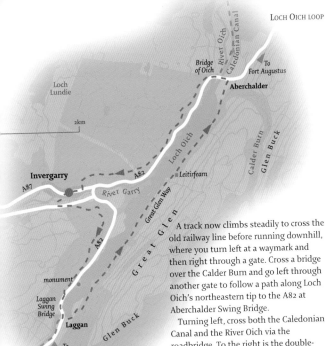

A track now climbs steadily to cross the old railway line before running downhill, where you turn left at a waymark and then right through a gate. Cross a bridge over the Calder Burn and go left through another gate to follow a path along Loch Oich's northeastern tip to the A82 at Aberchalder Swing Bridge.

Turning left, cross both the Caledonian Canal and the River Oich via the roadbridge. To the right is the double-cantilevered Bridge of Oich, opened in 1854, five years after floods destroyed the previous bridge.

Cross the entrance of a car park, then bear right onto a path which climbs above and then away from the A82. Walk for 2km to gain a track beside the A82, turning right onto this for a prolonged but gradual pull that leads high above Loch Oich and then Invergarry.

After 1.75km, take a waymarked path on the right and descend gradually through woodland to meet the A87 at Invergarry. Turn right and return to the start.

follow what is now a level, wooded path northeast above Loch Oich.

After around 1.5km, leave the track at a waymark to join a path which leads to the scenic shore. Beyond a gate, carry on through the Aberchalder Estate for 2km to reach the 18th-century red-roofed Leitirfearn Cottage. Leitirfearn translates as 'Hill of the Alders' and is a beautiful spot for a break – the distinctive golden-ringed dragonfly may be seen here during the summer.

◄ Loch Oich

75

Creag Meagaidh Nature Reserve

Distance 3km **Time** 1 hour
Terrain excellent paths throughout
Map OS Explorer 401 **Access** no public
transport to the start

Creag Meagaidh National Nature Reserve
has a range of habitats within its
boundaries, including mountain plateau
and upland glen. However, for those
wishing to explore the lower reaches of
the reserve then a short walk combining
the An Sidhean, Allt Dubh and
Alderwood Trails is perfect.

Start from the car park that sits on the
north side of the A86 near Aberarder. Take
the yellow waymarked An Sidhean Trail
which runs anti-clockwise to the left of
woodland and the Allt a' Chrannaig. An
Sidhean (pronounced 'Aan Shee-ann') is
Gaelic for 'the Fairies' and gives an
indication of the stories that were passed
down through generations by the people
who lived here. As you walk, keep an eye
out for chaffinch, greenfinch, brambling,
twite and reed bunting. Carry on easily

until the path culminates at a track.

Turn right here onto the red waymarked
Allt Dubh Trail ('the Black Stream') which
runs to the right of a track and continues
to the large white house of Aberarder.
Cross the track, then take a path to the
right of the house and climb gently
through birch and rowan woodland.

After crossing a footbridge over a burn,
views open up to the Creag Meagaidh
massif. In a while, the path rises a little
more steeply to a junction and a
viewpoint with the outlook extending
across Loch Laggan to Creag Pitridh and
Binnein Shuas.

Keep left and take the stony track which
bears left to run near the Allt Coire Ardair
alongside a strip of birch woodland.
Descend gently to a junction. On the right
is a bridge spanning what is now the Allt
Dubh, its clear, rapid waters tumbling
towards Loch Laggan. The riverbank is
lined with birch and rowan – watch out
for dipper and redpoll.

Turn left at the junction and walk

Creag Meagaidh

through open countryside to a fork where you take the right branch. A path drops easily down into more woodland with the buildings of Aberarder to the left. A short section of boardwalk leads back onto the path and to a fork.

Keep right onto the purple waymarked Alderwood Trail. This takes you through woodland comprised predominantly of alder but also with some birch, willow, rowan and holly. The alder trees here are unique as it is the only place in the Highlands where they have grown continuously for hundreds of years. Depending on the season, you will also find plenty of birdlife and wildflowers.

Cross a bridge over a burn to shortly exit the woodland, with the path now running to the right of a wildflower meadow where dragonflies, damselflies and butterflies can be seen in spring and summer. The trail soon re-enters the woods to pass a picnic bench beside the Allt Dubh, a good place to sit still and see what wildlife you can spy.

The path then veers left to run back alongside the wildflower meadow and on to the start.

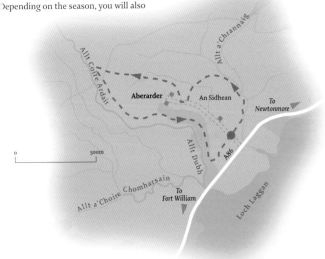

Coire Ardair

Distance **11.5km** Time **3 hours 30**
Terrain **excellent path throughout**
Map **OS Explorer 401** Access **no public transport to the start**

The teardrop-shaped Lochan a' Choire sits deep in the heart of the Creag Meagaidh National Nature Reserve and below the near vertical slopes of Coire Ardair (pronounced 'Ardour'). An out-and-back walk to the lochan travels through one of Scotland's most remarkable landscapes, allowing you to experience the wilder side of this reserve.

Start from the car park that sits on the north side of the A86 near Aberarder. Take the path marked with a red pine marten post and follow this west alongside oak woodland to a junction. Cross a track, then turn left and continue to reach a house at Aberarder. Cross back over the track, then take a path to the right of the house which rises gently through birch and rowan trees with fine views south across Loch Laggan.

In a while, the path climbs a little more steeply to a junction. Keep right at a fork, leaving the red waymarks. The path now rises north and then northwest under the slopes of Na Cnapanan and then Carn Liath with the whitewater of the Allt Coire Ardair roaring below – dozens of common spotted orchids line the path in summer.

The reserve has some of the most varied habitats in the Highlands, from arctic mountain plateau to rare alder woodland,

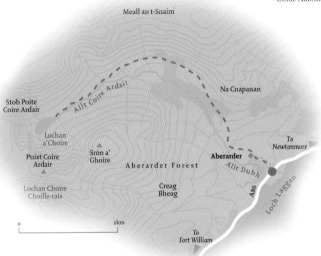

Meall an t-Snaim

Allt Coire Ardair

Na Cnapanan

Stob Poite
Coire Ardair

To
Newtonmore

Lochan
a'Choire

Sròn a'
Ghoire

Aberarder

Puist Coire
Ardair

Aberarder Forest

Allt Dubh

Lochan Choire
Choille-rais

Creag
Bheag

A86

Loch Laggan

0   2km

To
Fort William

with golden eagle, meadow pipit, dotterel, osprey, snow bunting, ptarmigan, wheatear, mountain hare and red deer just a selection of the wildlife to look out for at different times of year.

Once through a strip of birch woodland, the gradient eases and the path proceeds through the upland glen, home to Scots pine, bell heather, bilberry and purple moor grass. The flora becomes more alpine in character, with lady's mantle, crowberry, cowberry, starry saxifrage and mountain everlasting among the wildflowers you may be able to spot.

As the path then veers southwest, the view is dominated by Coire Ardair and its castellated cliffs. Drop steadily to walk alongside the sparkling Allt Coire Ardair, which journeys through Coire Ardair to

Loch Laggan. Brown trout and lamprey live in its fast-flowing waters, along with caddis fly, stonefly and water beetle larvae.

A gradual pull takes you above the river to approach Lochan a' Choire. The path comes to a halt above the shores of the lochan, which only appears at the last moment framed by Coire Ardair's bare, rugged cliffs rising almost 400m from the corrie floor and the crags of Stob Poite Coire Ardair.

For much of the winter, Lochan a' Choire is frozen and only a few water dwellers, such as freshwater shrimps, sticklebacks, brown trout and arctic char, can survive in such extreme conditions

This is the perfect location to simply sit quietly and see what wildlife you can spot before retracing your steps to the car park.

The Road to the Isles is one of the most celebrated stretches of highway in Scotland, winding its way from Fort William to Mallaig through a landscape filled with history, intrigue and romance.

Its early miles lead past Corpach, notable for its gleaming white lighthouse at the outflow of the Caledonian Canal which begins (or ends) its 96km journey here.

This part of Lochaber will be forever linked with Charles Edward Stuart and the Jacobite Uprising of 1745. Referred to by many at the time as the Young Pretender and better known today as Bonnie Prince Charlie, Charles famously raised the royal standard on the shores of Loch Shiel at Glenfinnan, beginning the revolt against the British monarchy. The Glenfinnan Monument, built to commemorate the event, forms the centrepiece of a picturesque walk around the viewpoints at the head of Loch Shiel.

All along the Road to the Isles are sites associated with the Young Pretender, including Fassfern, a little east of Glenfinnan. Here, riverbank and woodland paths combine to make a royal walk worthy of a prince.

Glenfinnan is also known for its magnificent viaduct completed in 1901, though it took another century to truly put it in the limelight with its brief but memorable appearance in the first *Harry Potter* movie. The viaduct is the focal point of a route that explores a magical landscape.

Further west, the Road to the Isles leads past Arisaig and a string of pristine white beaches. You'll want to linger at each and every one on a walk to Camusdarach.

As a final destination, it doesn't get much better than Mallaig with its quiet countryside, endless seascapes and a mouthwatering choice of seafood to sample at day's end. For some, this may whet the appetite for more distant adventures as it is here that you can hop aboard one of several ferries and set sail for Knoydart, Skye, Eigg or beyond.

The Road to the Isles

1 Towpath to Neptune's Staircase 82
There's admirable engineering ingenuity as well as a great view of Ben Nevis on this easy stroll

2 Fassfern and the pony track 84
A romantic woodland walk which starts where a prince once picked a rose before he picked a fight

3 Glenfinnan viewpoints 86
Take in an unforgettable view down Loch Shiel on a short walk that really raises the standard

4 Glenfinnan Viaduct 88
A wizard time is guaranteed on this circular potter to a spellbinding bit of railway architecture

5 The Strath of Arisaig 90
Explore a wooded glen before returning to a lovely lochside vista

6 Camusdarach beachcomber 92
Old Ben Knox was right – these sandy beaches are priceless

7 Mallaig and the Isles 94
It may be the end of the road, but there's still plenty to see!

Towpath to Neptune's Staircase

Distance 4.25km **Time** 1 hour 30
Terrain canal towpath **Map** OS Explorer 392
Access regular trains from Glasgow and
buses from Fort William to Corpach

Strung around the north shore of Loch
Linnhe, Corpach holds the perfect
position for viewing Ben Nevis across the
water. It is also the start (or end) of the
Caledonian Canal and this walk follows
the towpath along its banks before
climbing the famed Neptune's Staircase.

Begin from the car park beside the canal
at Corpach. Its somewhat melancholy
Gaelic translation is 'Corpse Place' as it was
where funeral processions between Fort
William and Annat used to rest. It is from

this distance that the sheer scale of Ben
Nevis, Britain's highest mountain, can
really be appreciated. It is a massive but
shapely mountain, dwarfing the town of
Fort William, which nestles at its base.

Cross the lock over the canal near the
lighthouse, which dates from 1913 and wa
once a storeroom and workhouse. Turn le
to follow the towpath east on its southern
bank, passing a number of vessels moore
here. The canal is lined with ash, oak,
birch, larch, Scots pine, beech and rowan,
with herons, geese and swans frequently
spotted along its waters.

The towpath makes for easy walking as
rises gently past the Corpach Double Lock
to a fork. Keep left to continue by the

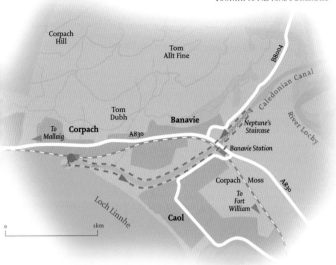

tranquil waters. Once through a gate, the towpath crosses a weir and in a short while veers left to run along the outskirts of Caol, with good views of the Mamores.

After 1.5km, the towpath approaches the A830. Before you get there, carefully go over a level crossing, passing through gates on either side to reach the Banavie Swing Bridge. Watch out for traffic as you cross the A830, then go through another gate back onto the towpath.

This now rises alongside the eight locks of Neptune's Staircase (also known as Banavie Locks), the greatest feat of engineering along the 96km-long Caledonian Canal. The staircase was named after the Roman god of the sea by the men who built the locks between 1803 and 1822.

Its 457m length makes it one of the longest set of locks in Britain. It was built to allow boats to rise or fall 19.5m and it takes about 1 hour 30 to pass through the entire Staircase. At first, 12 men were employed to open and close the locks, but since mechanisation during the 1960s this has reduced to only two.

At the top of the climb, cross the canal via the final lock and go left for a view along Loch Linnhe and over to Fort William. The towpath now drops back down to Banavie Swing Bridge.

Again be vigilant when going over the A830 and the level crossing before proceeding easily along the northern margin of the Caledonian Canal all the way back to Corpach.

◀ Ben Nevis from Corpach

Fassfern and the pony track

Distance 6km **Time** 2 hours
Terrain riverbank and forest paths and
tracks; one steep ascent and a sometimes
slippery descent **Map** OS Explorer 399
Access regular buses from Fort William
and Mallaig to Fassfern road end on A830

This walk begins from the hamlet of
Fassfern and follows the old Glen Loy
right of way through woodland and
alongside the An t-Suileag, a fast-flowing
river where kingfisher and dipper may be
spotted. There is one steep climb and a
descent which can be a little slippery after
periods of rain, but the paths are generally
good throughout with panoramas of the
big mountains of the West Highlands to
beckon you on.

Translating from Gaelic as 'Stance of the
Alder Trees', Fassfern sits just north of the
A830 around halfway along Loch Eil. There
is a small car park and information boards
beside the old stone bridge over the

An t-Suileag. Fassfern is reputedly where
Bonnie Prince Charlie picked a white rose
for his bonnet after raising the Jacobite
standard at Glenfinnan in 1745. The white
rose was one of several secret Jacobite
emblems; they also liked sunflowers (to
symbolise loyalty as they followed the
sun) and butterflies (which gloriously
emerged from their chrysalis, just as the
Stuarts would one day return to power).

From the car park, cross the bridge, then
turn left onto the Glen Loy Right of Way.
This old pony track was used to transport
charcoal to Loch Eil from a number of
charcoal burners that were spread out
along the glen. It runs to the right of the
river, winding gradually uphill through the
open countryside of Gleann Suileag, which
is scattered with oak and birch, mosses,
lichens and ferns. On the higher slopes are
conifers, which were planted in the 1950s.

The track drops back down to the clear
waters of the An t-Suileag and continues

◄ The bridge at Fassfern

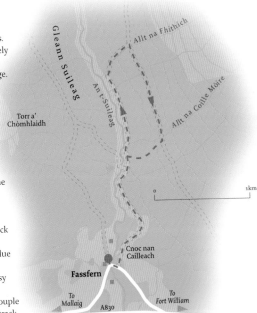

north along its banks. There are several lovely waterfalls as it flows down through a gorge. Look out for siskin, bullfinches, woodpeckers, crossbills, buzzards and dippers, with the glen also home to a range of butterfly species, including the globally threatened chequered skipper butterfly.

In a while, the track leads past a bridge. From here, follow blue waymarkers which carry on past a grassy track on the right.

After crossing a couple of footbridges, the track veers right before rising steadily to cross another footbridge where it forks. Keep right for a steep climb to soon gain a junction.

Walk right onto a track where tree-felling has resulted in sweeping views across Gleann Suileag and Loch Eil to the distinctive top of Stob Coire a' Chearcaill. As you head south the big, angular summits of the Moidart mountains are clearly visible to the west.

The track carries on for around 750m, crossing several footbridges to reach a blue waymark on the right. Here, a grassy path takes you down to a stony trail, which in turn drops steadily through conifer trees. It can be a little boggy but is, by and large, in good condition with views continuing along the glen.

Eventually, the path leads you back down to the outward route. Here, take a left and retrace your steps beside the An t-Suileag to Fassfern.

Glenfinnan viewpoints

Distance 4km **Time** 1 hour 30
Terrain woodland and hillside paths;
short, steady climbs **Map** OS Explorer 391
Access trains and buses from Fort
William and Mallaig to Glenfinnan

This simple walk visits the historic
Glenfinnan Monument and climbs to
several vantage points over the rough,
untamed landscape surrounding Loch
Shiel and the River Callop. In summer,
an abundance of birdlife, wildflowers
and dragonflies add to the appeal.

Begin from the National Trust for
Scotland Visitor Centre (open daily
between April and October) at Glenfinnan
where there is a small parking charge.

Take the path that leads up behind the
visitor centre and through a gate, with a
steady climb then swinging left to a
hillside viewpoint. Here, the Glenfinnan
Monument draws the eye down Loch
Shiel, a scene that is framed by steep,
craggy mountains. There is also a fine
view of St Mary's and St Finnan Church.

Walk back down to the visitor centre,
carefully cross the A830 and follow a path
to the monument, one of Scotland's most
iconic structures, topped by a statue of an
anonymous kilted Highlander. It marks
the spot where on 19 August 1745 Charles
Edward Stuart, better known as Bonnie
Prince Charlie, raised his standard to
begin the doomed uprising which ended
eight months later at Culloden.

The memorial was built in 1815 by
Alexander Macdonald of Glenaladale,
having been designed by the Scottish
architect James Gillespie Graham.

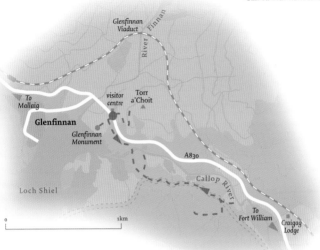

Glenfinnan Viaduct

River Finnan

visitor centre

Torr a'Choit

To Mallaig

Glenfinnan

Glenfinnan Monument

A830

Callop River

Loch Shiel

To Fort William

Craigag Lodge

0   1km

Retrace your steps again but, just before the A830, turn right onto a boardwalk signposted for Callop. Walk through a woodland of alder, willow, birch and Scots pine and carry on along a path once the boardwalk ends. At a fork, keep right and cross a bridge over the Callop River, which marks the boundary between Moidart and Ardgour. Look right for the remains of the Callop passenger ferry pier. The ferry transported passengers and supplies to local inhabitants on the banks of Loch Shiel between 1893 and the 1950s.

The bridge gives way to boardwalk, which extends for some distance through a peaceful landscape dotted with specimens of Scots pine to reach a forestry road. Turn left, then left again onto the 'Hilltop View' path. This climbs steadily up steps to gain the wooded top

of a low hill with another fine view of Loch Shiel and an outlook east to the bulky profile of Ben Nevis.

Return to the forestry road and carry on along this, heading to the left of a craggy hill (the next objective), as far as a 'Loch View' waymark after around 700m. Turn right here and climb a path through a gate for a gradual ascent over heathery slopes to the top of the crag. The outlook over Loch Shiel, Ben Nevis and the Aonachs is worth the small effort.

Head back down to the forestry road, joining it for a short climb before going left at a 'River View' waymark after about 100m. It is only a little way to this viewpoint, with the River Callop cutting its course through the landscape below.

Return to the forestry road and retrace your steps to Glenfinnan.

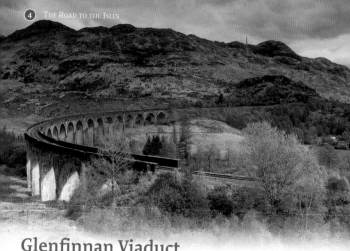

Glenfinnan Viaduct

Distance 4km **Time** 1 hour 30
Terrain well-maintained paths; one
steady climb **Map** OS Explorer 391
Access trains and buses from Fort
William and Mallaig to Glenfinnan

Although well over 100 years old, it took
the release of the first *Harry Potter* film in
2001 for the Glenfinnan Viaduct to receive
the mass recognition it richly deserves.
In *Harry Potter and the Philosopher's Stone*,
the Hogwart's Express can be seen
steaming across the bridge and granting
this iconic structure, for a fleeting
moment, centrestage. This route passes
under the bridge before climbing high
above Loch Shiel.

Begin from the National Trust for
Scotland Visitor Centre (open daily
between April and October) at Glenfinnan
where there is a small parking charge.

Carefully cross the A830 and turn right.
Follow the pavement over a bridge across
the River Finnan and then turn right onto
a minor road.

After passing a small car park, this quiet
road is easily followed through scenic
countryside towards the imposing
Glenfinnan Viaduct. Just before the
viaduct, turn left onto a stony track,
signposted for 'Glenfinnan Station
Museum and Sleeping and Dining Cars'.
Climb this for a few metres, then take a
path on the right and walk through an
archway beneath the bridge.

This magnificent structure has 21
arches, with the tallest being around 30m
in height, and it is 380m in length. It was
completed in 1901 as part of the extension
of the West Highland Railway from Fort
William to Mallaig, known as 'the Iron
Road to the Isles'.

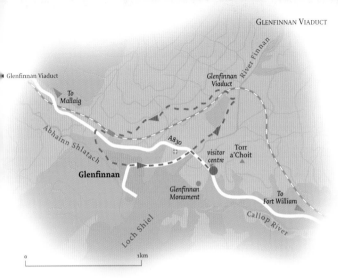

Walk through a gate with a good path now rising steadily up the lower slopes of Tom na h-Aire where views open out over the viaduct to the rocky slopes of Mam a' Chreagain. The trail then heads southwest away from the railway bridge and rises over a crest with an unexpected view along Loch Shiel – big mountains such as Sgurr Ghiubhsachain dominate the scene. The path is well maintained as it continues above the railway line and high above the loch, undulating through peaceful countryside.

Eventually it reaches a viewpoint above Glenfinnan Station. The path now zigzags down through a gate and onwards to the platform. Turn left, follow it to its end (the station office is on the other side) and carefully cross the line to reach the sleepers and dining car, which provide a

unique place for a meal and can sleep up to 10 people.

Glenfinnan Station opened in 1901 and today the station buildings are home to a fantastic museum, which was established in 1991 and details the history of the West Highland Railway.

Turn right and walk down the station entrance road to the A830. Carefully cross over, turn right and then, after a few metres, go left and drop down a track; this passes several houses before running alongside the Abhainn Shlatach. At a junction, turn left onto a minor road and follow this easily, keeping an eye out on the left for the small but perfectly formed St Mary's and St Finnan Church, which was built in 1873.

Continue back to the A830, turn right and return to the visitor centre.

The Strath of Arisaig

Distance 4.5km **Time** 1 hour 30
Terrain woodland tracks, minor roads
Map OS Explorer 398 **Access** regular trains
from Glasgow and buses from Fort
William and Mallaig to Arisaig

**The woodland and countryside of the
Strath of Arisaig sit quietly waiting to be
discovered beside the more renowned
coastal scenery of Arisaig. A pleasant and
easy stroll through the woods and along
the banks of Loch nan Ceall explores a
landscape that is rich in wildlife and
filled with memorable views.**

There is ample parking in Arisaig along
the shorefront of Loch nan Ceall. The loch
was the scene of a battle in 1746 when the
Royal Navy captured two French ships
sent to help the Jacobites after the Battle
of Culloden. However, the French escaped
with their bounty of gold and apparently
hid it near Loch Arkaig.

Facing the loch from the centre of the
village, turn left and follow the road past
the Land, Sea & Islands Centre, here
turning right onto the minor road for
Rhu. This narrow road makes its way
along the shore of the loch with views out
to the unmistakable profiles of the Isles
of Eigg and Rum.

Between March and July, Manx
shearwater may well be spotted here, as
might Minke whale between May and
September. Throughout the year, puffins,
seals, otters, harbour porpoise and
bottlenose dolphin are frequent visitors.

Cross a bridge over a narrow canal (this
was used to float timber from Mains Farm
sawmill into Loch nan Ceall), pass a metal
gate on the left, then turn left across a
cattle grid onto a track. With the canal to
your left, bear east towards Mains Farm
through the Strath of Arisaig, which is
cloaked in oak, beech and birch woodland

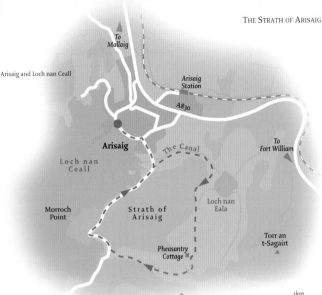

Arisaig and Loch nan Ceall

at puts on a spectacular display of olour in autumn. The Strath of Arisaig is haracteristically wide and shallow, ounded by rugged little hills as it tretches east to Druimindarroch.

After the track curves right, follow it ast the farmhouse, go through a gate nd pass several farm buildings. Beyond nother gate, the track continues through eautiful countryside with Loch nan Eala Loch of the Swans') in view on the left; ere, you may spy reed bunting, sedge varbler and yellowhammer, as well as a ne of small rugged hills to the south.

Carry on, skirting more oak and birch voodland to meet a junction beside a vhitewashed cottage. Turn left here to ollow another track towards a large nouse. Just before this, turn right at a crossroads and proceed easily along a track through attractive countryside. The wooded slopes of Druim an Dubh-leathaid ('the Ridge of the Dark Hillside') rise steeply to the left.

After crossing a cattle grid, the track drops gently back to the minor road for Rhu beside the secluded bay of Camus an t-Salainn. Turn right to take this quiet road, flanked by birch, oak, hazel and rowan, sweeping right past Morroch Point to continue northeast, passing a number of houses.

The road then runs alongside Loch nan Ceall, with views over to Eigg and Rum as you eventually rejoin the outward route and retrace your steps to Arisaig.

Camusdarach beachcomber

Distance 13km **Time** 4 hours
Terrain rough coastal paths, beach, quiet
roads **Map** OS Explorer 398 **Access** regular
trains from Glasgow and buses from Fort
William and Mallaig to Arisaig

The west coast of Scotland is renowned
for its string of silver beaches and
mesmerising seascapes. Nowhere is this
better seen than in the four glorious
miles between the village of Arisaig and
the undisturbed beauty of Camusdarach
Beach which bookend this simple walk.
Camusdarach is an arc of brilliant white
sand with the intense blue waters of the
Sound of Sleat drawing the eye to the
Small Isles and Skye's jagged contours.

Begin from the village of Arisaig where
there is ample parking. In the early 19th
century, Arisaig was home to a thriving
community with both fishing and
crofting key to the village's economy.

However, like much of the Scottish
Highlands, it was shattered by the 18th
and 19th century land clearances. More
than 1000 Arisaig crofters were compelled
to leave their homes as landowners felt
that sheep were more economically viable
than people. Many of the crofters left for
Nova Scotia.

Facing Loch nan Ceall from the centre of
the village, turn right and follow the
B8008 through Arisaig, taking the chance
to look out for some of the marine life
that is seen in these waters, including
harbour porpoise and bottlenose dolphin.

As the road sweeps right, turn left onto
a minor road signposted for Arisaig
Cemetery. Follow this to a small car park,
turn right through a gate and then climb a
path into the grounds of St Mary's Church
with its flat-topped tower. The present-
day structure dates from 1849.

Exit the grounds through a gate and

Isles of Eigg and Rum from Camusdarach

turn left onto the B8008, following this for 1.25km (it's a quiet road, but keep an eye out for traffic all the same) to a junction. Keep left to continue on the B8008 with views out to Skye as you head downhill past Back of Keppoch to reach the entrance to Invercaimbe Caravan Site after 750m.

Turn left and follow a track through the site to Caimbe Beach. From here, the route bears north over brilliant sands and around rocky coves, passing another small campsite. The landscape never fails to inspire and the keen-eyed may even spot a sea eagle.

A rougher path skirts the rugged Portnaluchaig and its campsite, before you take to the beach alongside the B8008 to reach the scattering of houses at Traigh, home to what must be Scotland's most idyllic golf course.

Keep north along the coast with a mixture of soft sand and grassy paths taking you the final mile to Camusdarach, an idyllic spot to unwind and bask in a breathtaking seascape that includes the Isles of Eigg, Rum and Skye before – reluctantly – making the return journey.

Some scenes for the classic 1983 Scottish movie *Local Hero* were filmed here it was the setting for the ramshackle home of the beach scavenger hermit Ben Knox, the character played by Scottish actor Fulton MacKay), as well as the popular television series *Hamish Macbeth*, starring Robert Carlyle. The beach is a popular setting for marriages.

Either retrace your steps along the coast or make the short hop over the dunes and through a car park to pick up the B8008 and follow this back to Arisaig.

Mallaig and the Isles

Distance 3.25km **Time** 1 hour
Terrain pavement, minor roads,
countryside paths **Map** OS Explorer 398
Access regular trains from Glasgow and
buses from Fort William to Mallaig

**Mallaig is situated at the end of the
Rathad nan Eilean, or Road to the Isles,
where a number of ferries sail from the
harbour bound for the remote peninsula
of Knoydart and the isles of Skye, Eigg,
Muck, Canna and Rum. This short walk
explores the harbourside before diving
into a secluded glen.**

Turn right from the railway station onto
Station Road and walk through the town
centre. The name Mallaig possibly derives
from the Old Norse *Muli*, meaning
'Headland Bay', and its deep and sheltered
harbour beside the Sound of Sleat has
accounted for its development as a port.
Not surprisingly, fishing has been the

cornerstone of Mallaig's growth since
1841 when Lord Lovat, the owner of North
Morar Estate, parcelled up the farmstead
of Mallaigvaig into a series of plots to
attract people to settle here, with fishing
being the main occupation.

With the arrival of the railway in 1901,
and the steamers sailing for Skye and the
Hebrides, Mallaig subsequently became a
popular visitor destination.

Continue around Mallaig Harbour along
East Bay, passing the line of waterside
parking spaces at East Bay Car Park to
reach a second car park by the same name.
Opposite this, to the left of a whitewashed
cottage, is a narrow path signposted
'Circular Walk'.

Take this to go through a gate, after
which the path climbs steadily away from
the town and up a hillside. As it swings
left at a bench, views open out across
Mallaig. Keep climbing gradually with

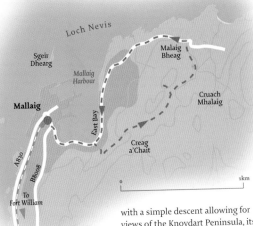

Mallaig Harbour

Loch Nevis

Sgeir
Dhearg

Malaig
Bheag

Mallaig
Harbour

Cruach
Mhalaig

Mallaig

East Bay

Creag
a'Chait

A830

B8008

To
Fort William

0   1km

with a simple descent allowing for views of the Knoydart Peninsula, its tiny community of Inverie dwarfed by several huge mountains, including Ladhar Bheinn and Luinne Bheinn.

Reaching a track beside a white cottage, turn left and follow this through Malaig Bheag (Little Mallaig) onto a narrow paved road and past a few cottages, with panoramic views across to Knoydart persisting. At a junction, keep left onto Mallaig Vaig Road and follow this, with an outlook to Skye's celebrated mountains, as it drops down to Mallaig's rugged coast. It then runs alongside several houses to a junction.

Turn right and then sweep left onto East Bay. This is easily followed back into town where the option to sample some seafood in one of several excellent eateries is a fine way to end the walk.

steep slopes to the right to reach a fork.

Branch right and follow the path into a secluded glen, bounded on either side by steep embankments and scattered with wildflowers during spring and summer. This soon rises to a crossroads. Go left and take a path which climbs a short, steep slope. At the top is a stunning view across the Sound of Sleat to the Isle of Eigg's distinctive high point, the Sgurr of Eigg, the spiky Rum Cuillin and the serrated outline of Skye's Black Cuillin. The more rounded range known as the Red Cuillin is also clearly visible. This is an ideal spot to watch the ferries from and enjoy a picnic.

Return to the main path and continue

Index

Achriabhach Forest Trail 56
Altnafeadh 12
Am Bodach 12, 14
An Torr 18
Aonach Eagach 14, 18
Ardgour 32
Ardgour Peninsula 42
Ardnamurchan Lighthouse 38
Ardnamurchan Peninsula 36
Arisaig 90, 92
Ariundle Oakwood 34
Ba Cottage 8
Ballachulish 24, 26
Beinn a' Chrulaiste 10
Ben Hiant 36
Ben Nevis 52, 54, 56, 58, 64, 82
Blackrock Cottage 8
Brecklet Trail, The 26
Caledonian Canal, The 70, 72, 74, 82
Camusdarach 92
Camusnagaul 42
Castle Tioram 40
Charles Inglis Clark Memorial Hut 64
Clachaig Inn 18
Clovullin 32
Coire Ardair 78
Commando Memorial 68
Corpach 82
Corran 32
Cow Hill 48
Creag Meagaidh 76, 78
Crofter's Wood, The 42
Devil's Staircase, The 12
Dun Deardail 54
Fassfern 84
Fort William 46, 48
Gairlochy 70
Gleann Suileag 84
Glen Nevis 48, 50, 52, 54, 56, 58

Glencoe 8, 10, 12, 14, 16, 18, 20, 22
Glencoe Folk Museum 20, 22
Glencoe Lochan 22
Glencoe Village 20, 22
Glenfinnan 86, 88
Great Glen Way, The 70, 72, 74, 82
Grey Mare's Tail 28
High Bridge 68
Invergarry 74
Inverlochy Castle 46
Killiechonate Woodlands 66
Kingshouse Hotel 10
Kinlochleven 28
Laggan Locks 72
Loch Achtriochtan 18
Loch Moidart 40
Loch Leven 20, 22, 24, 28
Loch Linnhe 32, 42, 48, 82
Loch Lochy 70, 72, 74
Loch nan Ceall 90
Loch Oich 74
Loch Shiel 86, 88
Lost Valley, The 16
Mallaig 94
Moy Bridge 70
Neptune's Staircase 82
Pap of Glencoe, The 20, 22
Point of Ardnamurchan, The 38
Portuairk 38
Rathad nan Eilean 94
Ring of Steall, The 60
River Nevis, The 50, 52
River Shiel, The 40
Signal Rock 18
Spean Bridge 66, 68
Steall Gorge 58, 60
Strontian 34
West Highland Way, The
8, 10, 12, 28, 50, 54